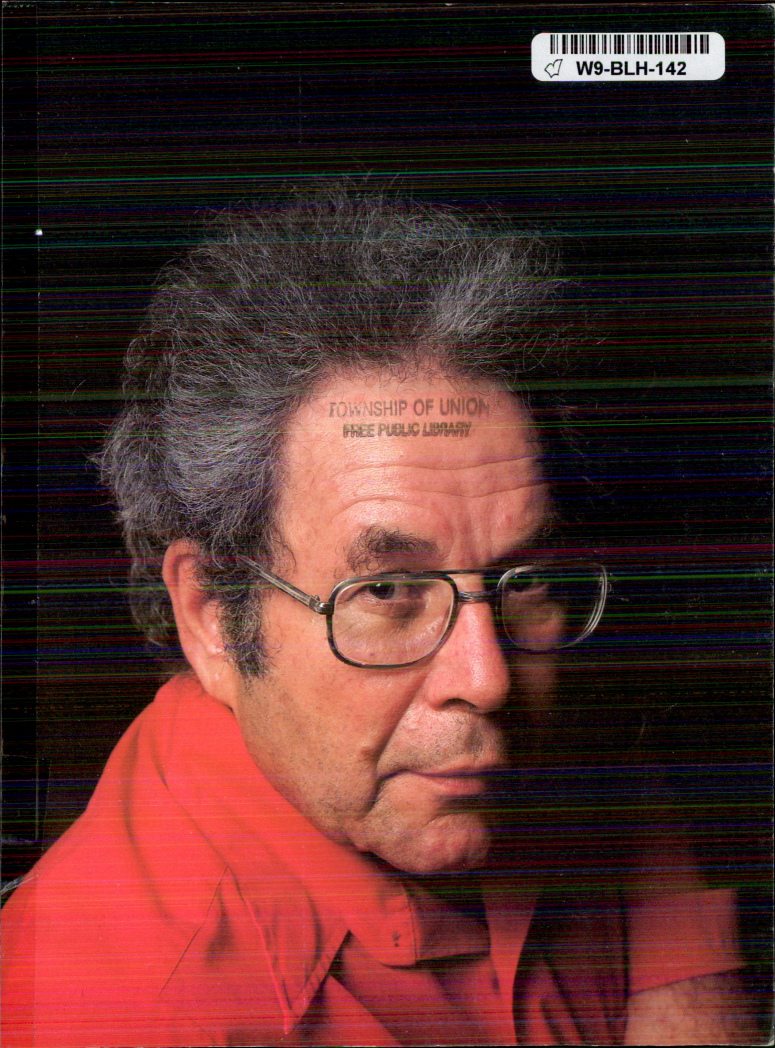

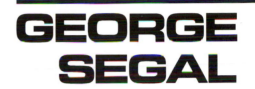

GEORGE
SEGAL

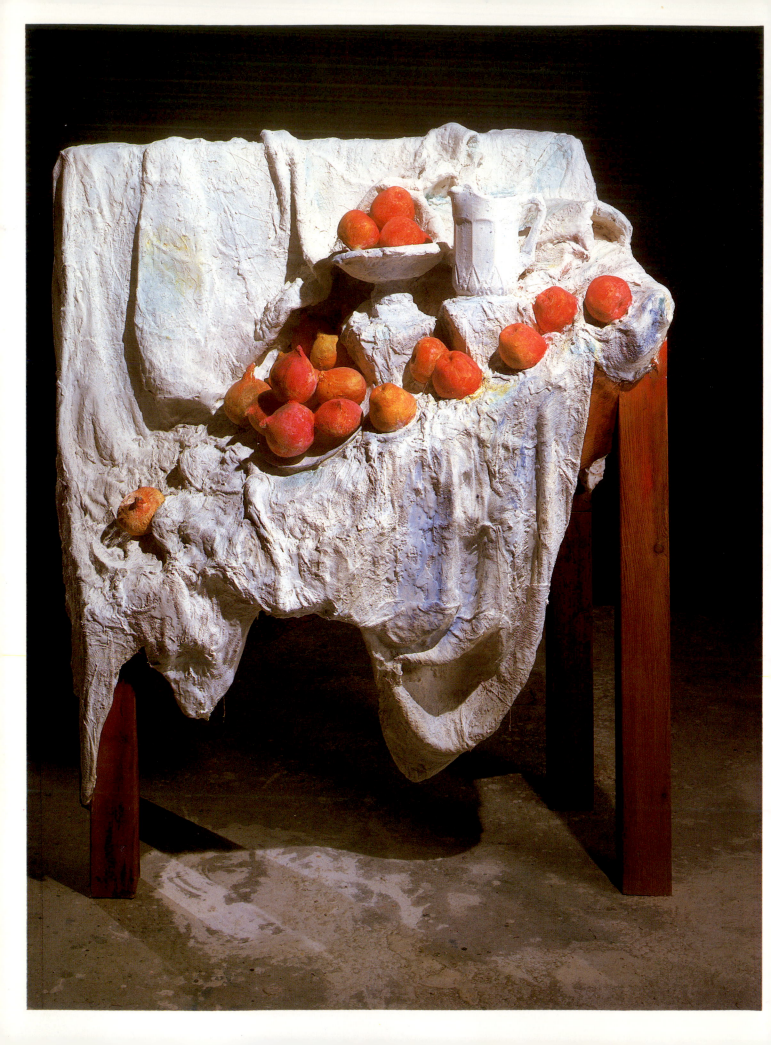

MODERN MASTERS

GEORGE SEGAL

PHYLLIS TUCHMAN

Abbeville Press · Publishers
New York · London · Paris

George Segal is volume five in the Modern Masters series.

ACKNOWLEDGMENTS: Many people made this book possible. Advice I received from Professor Hellmut Wohl when I was writing about George Segal at Boston University was still valuable years later. Alice Sedgwick Wohl also offered pertinent suggestions then and now. Angela Westwater, Peter Wolff, and Fran Lipton over the past year answered many practical questions that arose while this book was in preparation. About aspects of Segal's career with which they were familiar, Richard Bellamy, Alfred Leslie, Roy Lichtenstein, Nancy Rosen, and Michael Sonnabend consented to be interviewed. Sybil-Ann Sherman helped type the manuscript. For more than fifteen years, my parents, Evelyn and Jack Tuchman, and my sister, Dr. Gaye Tuchman, have encouraged my study of this remarkable artist. Above all, to George and Helen Segal, two lovely people, I am grateful for the conversations and meals we have enjoyed together since 1967.

FRONT COVER: *The Dancers*, 1971–82. See plate 48.
BACK COVER: *Man Walking along Brick Wall*, 1988. Painted plaster, wood, and plastic-tempered hardboard, 100 x 84 x 30 in. Private collection; courtesy Sidney Janis Gallery, New York.
ENDPAPERS: George Segal, 1983. Photographs by Michael Abramson.
FRONTISPIECE: *Cézanne Still Life #4, 1981.* Painted plaster, wood, and metal, 57 x 48 x 24 in. Courtesy Sidney Janis Gallery, New York.

Series design by Howard Morris
Editor: Nancy Grubb
Designer: Gerald Pryor
Picture Editor: Christopher Sweet
Production Manager: Dana Cole
Chronology, Exhibitions, Public Collections, and Selected Bibliography compiled by Anna Brooke

Marginal numbers in the text refer to works illustrated in this volume.

Library of Congress Cataloging-in-Publication Data

Tuchman, Phyllis.
  George Segal.
  (Modern master series, ISSN 0738-0429; v. 5)
  Bibliography: p.
  Includes index.
  1. Segal, George, 1924–. 2. Sculptors—United States—Biography. I. Title. II. Series.
NB237.S44T8 1983 730'.92'4 83-3858
ISBN 0-89659-328-2
ISBN 1-55859-255-5 (pbk.)

First edition, 15 14 13 12 11 10 9 8 7 6 5 4

Contents

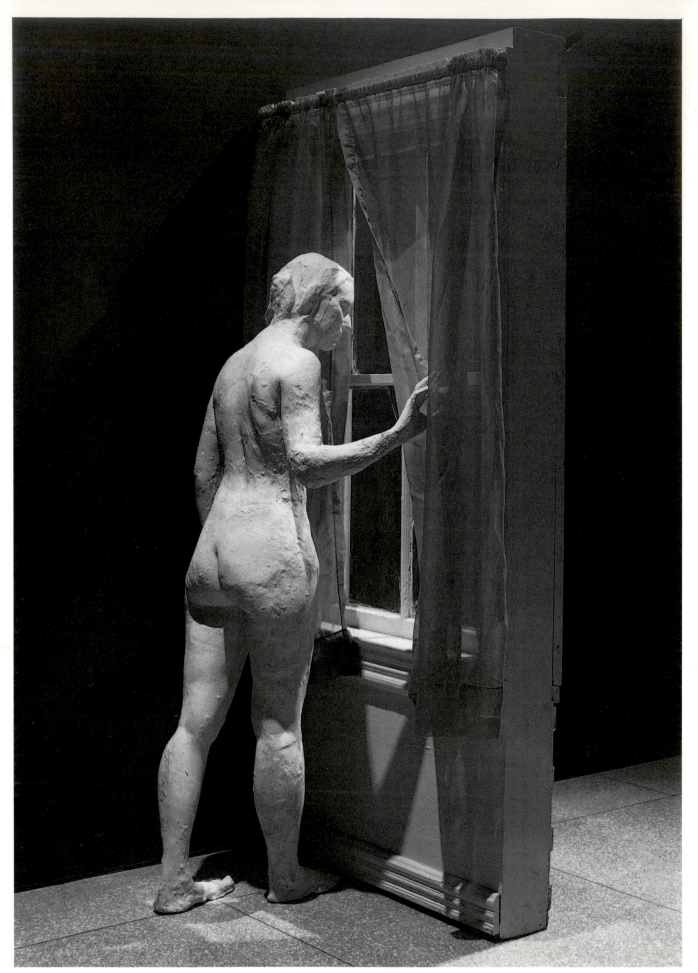

Introduction

For more than twenty years, George Segal has begun his sculptures by wrapping friends, relatives, and models in plaster-soaked bandages. This technique has proven to be astonishingly fertile. Pliant, hollow forms have served as the basis for several hundred single and multifigure compositions as well as scores of body-part fragments.

Initially, the white surfaces were always left bare; today, most are colored and frequently bear more than a passing resemblance to the second-generation Abstract Expressionist canvases that Segal made throughout the 1950s and into the 1960s. Often both the ghostly and the tinted characters interact with objects in environmental situations in which their poses seem utterly natural and lifelike. Three pedestrians wait on a corner while a street light blinks, "Walk, Don't Walk." Two lovers embrace on a bed. A naked woman gazes through a curtained window.

Although it is the realistic aspects of Segal's art—the figures and their surroundings—that first attract a viewer's attention, the sculptures are developed formally according to the principles of twentieth-century abstraction. Upon further reflection, it becomes clear that the artist seeks to evoke either a philosophical or psychological truth about his models and their actions. One is either seduced at first glance by these works or else one dismisses them just as readily. But the viewer who is intrigued will be rewarded by the opportunity to ponder a broad range of interests and issues.

Segal is fascinated by human relationships. Works with only one character seated by a window or standing by a door often communicate a harrowing loneliness. But many of his other scenes consist of multiple figures that relate to each other according to the situation at hand. People gather around a dinner table or wait to board a bus. *The Brick Wall* (1970) vividly illustrates how much Segal can convey with a simple gesture. The married couple who posed for it—a psychiatrist and a painter—seem merely to walk side-by-side along a brick wall when they are seen head-on. The way the doctor's left arm is wrapped around his wife's waist is visible only when the pair is viewed from the rear, but it is this subtle gesture that reveals the bonding in their relationship.

When talking about his work, Segal will refer to its various

1. *The Curtain*, 1974
Plaster, wood, fabric, and glass, 84 x 39 x 32 in.
National Museum of American Art,
Smithsonian Institution, Washington, D.C.

levels of meaning. Political consciousness, for example, has been integrated into certain environments from early in his career to the present. *The Bus Riders* was made in 1962 at the height of the activities of the Freedom Riders in the Deep South. *The Execution* appeared in 1967 when teach-ins and sit-ins against the Vietnam War were rampant on college campuses. More recently, *Gay Liberation*, a bronze of 1980, treats another subject not commonly associated with the fine arts. Just as surprisingly, Segal has also produced a number of sculptures that reflect upon the teachings of the Torah. In works like *The Legend of Lot*, *The Sacrifice of Isaac*, and *The Holocaust* he has endeavored to deal with present-day questions of morality.

In yet another group of sculptures, Segal has made art about art in unexpected ways. He adores Mondrian. In many of his early works, Segal balanced form and color in environments as if he were creating a three-dimensional abstract picture by using realistic elements instead of lines and planes. In 1967 he actually included a painting by Mondrian in a portrait of Segal's art dealer, Sidney Janis. Eleven years later, he wittily fashioned a plastic ceiling in *The Hot Dog Stand* as if it were an ersatz canvas by the early modern master.

2. *The Curtain*, front view. See plate 1

3. *The Brick Wall*, 1970
Plaster, wood, and plastic, 96 x 144 x 96 in.
National Museum of Art, Osaka

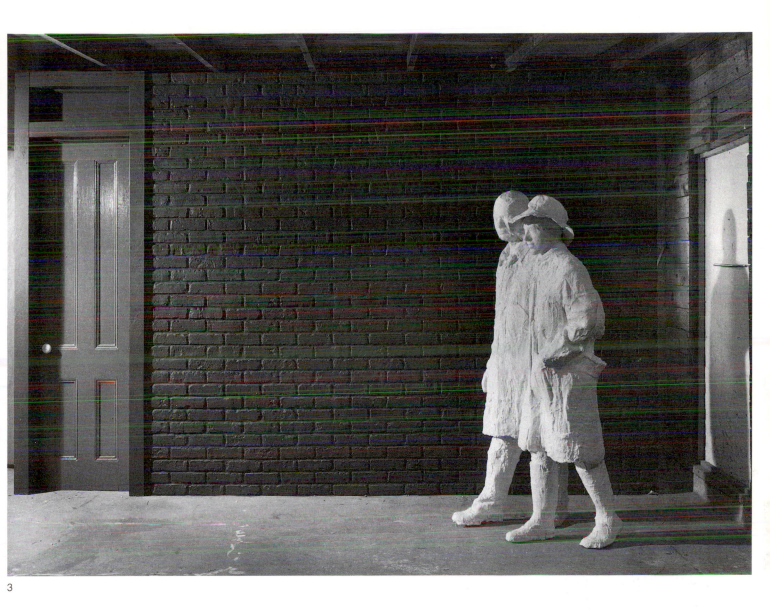

3

George Segal—a bespectacled, bushy-haired man of fifty-nine who generally wears comfortable, rumpled clothing—loves to tell a good story and to analyze philosophical questions with old friends and new acquaintances. As an art student during the late 1940s, he was trained by leading abstractionists of the day. He came to public attention during the early 1960s with his life-size plaster figures set among actual chairs and tables. Now, with a considerable body of work behind him; several retrospective exhibitions mounted in major museums throughout the United States, Europe, and Japan; books published about his work; and a Michael Blackwood documentary broadcast by PBS, Segal receives an increasing number of public commissions in bronze. Unsought notoriety has surrounded several of these projects, while others have been heartily embraced. (When *The Steelmakers* was installed in Youngstown, Ohio, he was given the key to the city.) While Segal speaks of having been "burned" on several occasions, he asserts, "If the opinions expressed about art are bland, more than likely the art lacks bite and perception."[1]

101

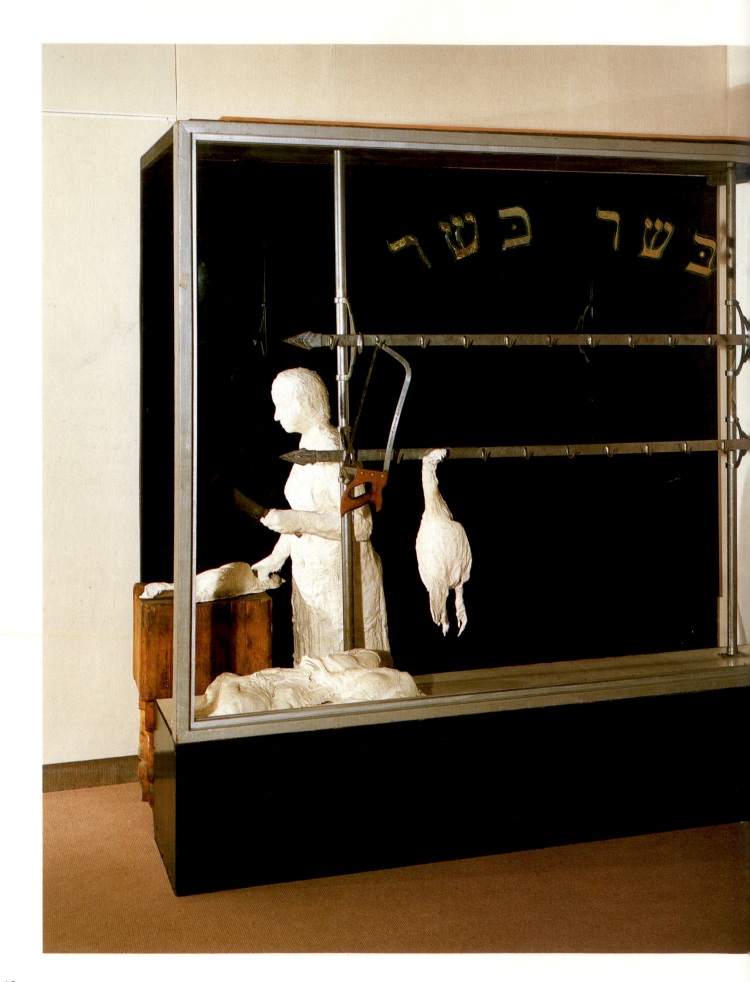

1 Background

Segal—on the surface, a mild-mannered Clark Kent; in action, a champion of the disenfranchised, the lonely, and the overlooked—has almost always lived forty-five minutes from the Museum of Modern Art. He was born in November 1924 in the Bronx, and grew up there. His father, Jacob, operated a kosher butcher store on 174th Street, just east of the Concourse. In 1965, six months after his father died, the sculptor memorialized him with *The Butcher Shop*, one of his most acclaimed pieces. Discussing the scene in which his mother, Sophie, is about to kill a chicken as she stands behind a broad window marked with Hebrew lettering, Segal has noted that the Orthodox ritual of slaughtering animals "announces obedience to God's laws. The Jews are famous for drenching most acts of daily life with inordinate weight."[2]

Segal realized that he wanted to become an artist when he was still in grammar school. "I liked the idea of making marks and scribbles," he recalled not too long ago.[3] After P.S. 70, he attended the newly opened Stuyvesant High School, producer of several Nobel Prize winners and today still an elite science academy. "I took all the entrance tests. They said I was undisciplined and scratchy and scrawly; but, I scored high in scientific aptitude. Being sent to Stuyvesant was too great an honor for me to resist." But once there, he majored in art, one of the many contradictions that have cropped up in his life.

In 1940, when Segal was in his senior year, his father bought a chicken farm in South Brunswick, New Jersey, on land across the road from where the sculptor and his wife of thirty-seven years, the former Helen Steinberg, continue to live. Segal remained in New York with an aunt to finish high school. Then he commuted from New Jersey to Cooper Union in lower Manhattan, where he had been accepted after passing another battery of rigorous qualifying examinations. He signed up for fine arts, but told his father he was enrolled in a commercial arts program. A year later, the war broke out. When his brother, Morris, was drafted, the younger son had to leave school to help support the family.

Segal spoke recently about the spirit of America during the 1930s and '40s, comparing his generation to the protesting college students of the 1960s. "My generation had a different mark on it," he said, "because just about everybody was willing to fight Hitler. There was unanimity, a singleness of purpose in the United States during World War II and before that, during the Depression, strangely enough. When I was a young kid, I remember everybody struggling or insecure or anxious about jobs being very scarce. But the streets were safe, and everybody agreed to play by the rules. Everybody thought they were in it together. There was a sense of extended family. It shattered after the War. The period you're recalling was a disintegration into individual ego, self-gratification, and loss of identity to something outside of yourself or your body or your own sensations. My generation carries a memory of another set of attitudes." In these recollections, one can glimpse the origins of the Everyman the artist so skillfully encases in plaster.

Twenty-two and married, Segal returned to school in 1947. He now studied art education at Pratt Institute in Brooklyn, but was not happy with his choice of school. Becoming more and more aware of the contemporary art scene in New York, then on the verge of replacing Paris as the center for painters and sculptors, Segal saw an exhibition of student work from New York University. "There was Abstract Expressionism, though I didn't even know the term," he has said. In 1948 he transferred to the university's art education department, based in Washington Square, and was awarded a B.S. the following year. His teachers were Tony Smith (at that time a practicing architect and painter, whose fame as a Minimalist sculptor came only years later) and William Baziotes (a New York School artist who died in 1963). Segal gives these two men, whom he recalls fondly, the credit for exposing him "to all the other Abstract Expressionist giants."

The postwar years were a special time to study art at N.Y.U. What had been a staid program training artists to become teachers had been transformed into an open classroom situation where returning veterans could collect their G.I. benefits while actively pursuing careers as exhibiting artists. In this environment, Segal was buffeted by ideas and troubled about how to deal with them in his paintings; he was also, and not incidentally, troubled about how to make a living for his family, which would soon include a son, Jeffrey, born in 1950, and a daughter, Rena, born in 1953. "My teachers," he says, "wanted me to paint the way they were painting. But they were talking about a totality of experience that involved the movies; literature; philosophy; the relationship between cultures; modern, outrageously avant-garde painting; old-fashioned, art historical stuff. They presented this entire mix to me and then they said, 'Work in a severely restricted fashion.' I decided that I wanted my work to express the entire spectrum that my teachers were talking about. Yes, I was interested in ethics. Yes, I was interested in literary subject matter. Yes, I was interested in form. I wanted all those elements to work together and oppose each other." It took Segal years to achieve this.

Some people thought he would never make it. When asked what Segal was like in those days, an old friend of his responded, "I remember him as a very preoccupied and troubled person who was trying to be an artist while he was running a functioning

4. *The Butcher Shop*, 1965 (pp. 10–11)
Plaster, wood, vinyl, metal, and plexiglass, 94 x 99 x 49 in.
Art Gallery of Ontario, Toronto
Gift from the Women's Committee Fund, 1966

5. *Model in Studio*, 1956
Oil on canvas, 60 x 48 in.
J. and R. Kutliroff

chicken farm. I didn't think he'd be able to continue making art because his difficulties were so pressing at the time." To his credit, Segal persevered, and when he started to make sculpture, he celebrated people who work hard and enjoy modest pleasures. Andy Warhol shows us our idols; Segal shows us ourselves.

Upon graduation, Segal settled down to run his own chicken farm. He spent six months building coops, and stopped painting for a few years. As the farm started to go sour, he began to consider teaching as a more viable profession. He was also making art again. Indeed, the oil paint was still wet on the new canvases when he met Allan Kaprow, a charismatic personality who had just accepted a position as art historian at Rutgers University in New Brunswick, New Jersey. As Segal puts it, "That woke up the whole infection/affection for art again."

The two men had friends in common. Kaprow had also gone to N.Y.U. and had, in addition, taken painting classes with Hans Hofmann, one of the most influential art teachers of the twentieth century, and studied at Columbia University with Meyer Schapiro, an equally legendary art historian. Reviewing an exhibition that Kaprow held at the Hansa Gallery in 1954, Fairfield Porter remarked upon the influences of Kirchner, the Fauves, and Pollock.

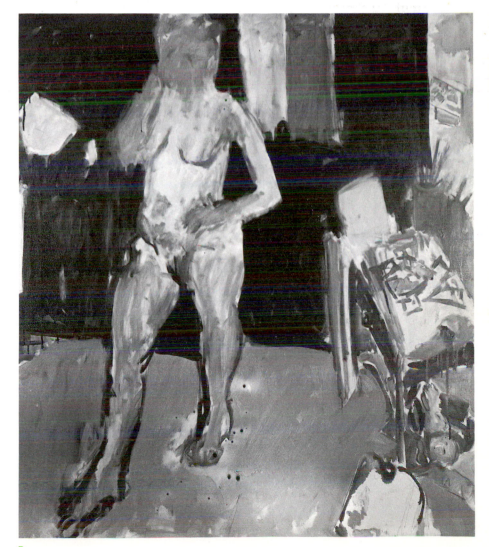

Segal would spend the next couple of years similarly grappling with a combination of inspirations from German Expressionism, the French Fauves, and Abstract Expressionism.

Segal was once again in touch with what was going on in New York galleries and museums. And he loved to listen to Kaprow talk about the ideas that led to his Happenings. "That was the magic explosion—a new way of looking at the real world," Segal says. He had long been struggling for a way to make art that would be figurative, yet would also employ the principles of abstraction and communicate philosophical notions. Under Kaprow's direction, Segal realized that "real objects take on a magical quality if you start introducing ideas that come from Duchamp, Schwitters, Italian Futurism, plus some kind of projection of modern, industrial society. We connected those ideas with the industrial landscape in New Jersey."

In 1957, and during the next seven years, Segal taught English and fine as well as industrial arts at nearby junior and senior high schools and adult education at local community centers. He also exhibited annually at the Hansa Gallery, a cooperative named for both Hans Hofmann and the Hanseatic League, a medieval federation of free towns familiar to the artist-members who had emigrated from Germany to America. By the time Segal joined the Hansa in the mid-1950s, the gallery had moved from East Twelfth Street to the parlor floor of a brownstone on Central Park South. Allan Kaprow was one of the original members. Others included Jan Muller, Wolf Kahn, Felix Pasilis, Richard Stankiewicz, Jean Follett, and Miles Forst.

Today, one of the most admired Hansa members is all but forgotten: Jean Follett. An exhibition she held during the spring of 1956 met with particular success. Curator Dorothy Miller bought a piece for the Museum of Modern Art, and art historian Leo Steinberg reviewed the show in *Arts Magazine*. Follett had used white and black to cover 48-by-60-inch Masonite boards, to which she attached metals and coals and coils. Steinberg observed that "these nine recent works [by Follett] are not quite paintings, though there's paint on them; they are not quite collages, though all kinds of *objets trouvés* are pasted down on the panels; and they are not quite constructions, though many elements project in full relief. . . ."[4] In terms of George Segal's development, Steinberg's highest praise of Follett's work must have been meaningful: "And lastly—the supreme antinomy—the outrageous modernity of the method and the classic balance, the almost academic probity of the design."[5]

In those days Kaprow too was pursuing an art that asserted material presence. An exhibition he held at the Hansa in 1957 included redolent hangings. (He had worked with a chemist to research odors that could be soaked into cloth.) Some were quite large; several had black letters collaged onto them. One work had particular bearing on Segal's future endeavors: *Woman Out of Fire*, a pendulous-breasted, three-dimensional figure cut off at her elbows and knees, made from roofing cement. She was one of several "tar-baby sculptures" by Kaprow. There was also a male figure made from welded pipes coated with tar. These provided

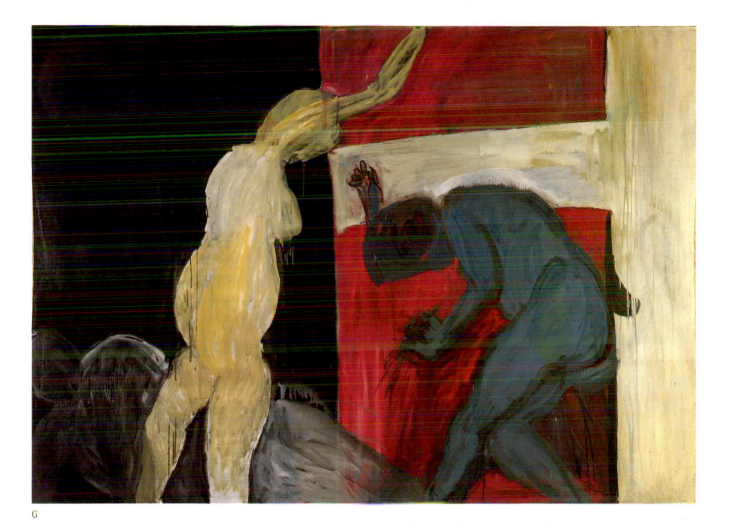

6

6. *The Blow*, 1958
Oil on canvas, 72 x 96 in.
Collection of the artist

inspiration for the early reliefs of Claes Oldenburg, and they were models for Segal. Today, Segal says, "Kaprow was a catalyst. He's been kicked aside, but I think he had a lot of influence, and provoked a lot of ideas. Besides, I like him personally."

In those days, Segal was a painter, and much influenced by Muller, Kahn, and Pasilis. His canvases were large, expressively colored studies with haunting, roughly outlined figures. (Once, toward the end of this period, the artist's wife was called in for a conference with an elementary school teacher who was troubled about their daughter's crayon drawings of people with purple faces and green hair. Helen Segal, normally not at a loss for words, did not know how to tell the teacher that that was what the child's father was doing too.)

Segal's first solo exhibition, held during February and March of 1956, featured festively painted nude studio models, still lifes, and interiors. A palette of primaries predominated. In a review in *Arts Magazine*, novelist and poet Barbara Guest praised "the freshness of color" in Segal's pictures, and noted how *At Work* reminded her of Matisse's *Studio*.[6] Nevertheless she was disappointed that there were occasional muddy passages, a trait not uncommon among second-generation Abstract Expressionists.

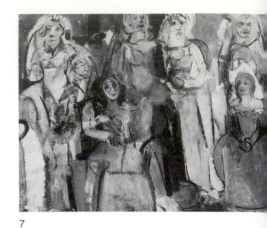

7

During the spring of 1957 Segal got his big break. Meyer Schapiro included his *Provincetown Interior* in *The New York School: Second Generation* at the Jewish Museum. In the introduction to the catalog, Leo Steinberg observed about canvases like Segal's: "Still lifes belie their names to look like upheavals, and all apparatus of table and kitchen sink confesses to a disturbed, enforced coexistence. . . ."[7] Together with work by Alfred Leslie, Kaprow, Follett, and four other Hansa members, this benchmark exhibition also included early works by Helen Frankenthaler, Joan Mitchell, Jasper Johns, and Robert Rauschenberg. There was another artist there

7 who particularly influenced Segal: Grace Hartigan. In her *Grand Street Brides*, a de Kooningesque rendering of a storefront window with mannequins dressed in wedding gowns, she synthesized figuration and abstraction in just the way Segal was after.

Segal held his next show in May 1957. These canvases were developed around the theme of partially clad figures. Nudes were wrapped in coats, capes, and cloaks. Space was defined by blankets of color. The artist was dealing deftly now with formal properties; but he was starting to wonder how he could include more volumetric figures and deeper space. Such concerns would soon lead him to produce three-dimensional art.

Elizabeth Pollet, an *Arts Magazine* reviewer, singled out "the expressive posture" of the figures depicted in Segal's latest paintings.[8] She also spoke of "an arc of physical tension as well as psychological focus," something Segal would later continue to achieve in his sculptures. Pollet, however, found the atmosphere "so rich and so solid," that she felt it made the figures "seem weak." *Artnews* critic Parker Tyler noticed that Segal had "intensified his already vivid palette. . . . His special *goût* for color and surface tension is already an accomplished thing."[9] Besides reacting to formal considerations, Tyler noted an aspect of Segal's art that is still evident: "a humility that ought to be exemplary."

In Segal's show at the Hansa in February–March 1958, nude figures were monumental; landscapes were filled with light. According to contemporary critics, the canvases reflected both expressionist and colorist sources—Soutine, Matisse, and Kokoschka. As Segal began to develop his art more from his own resources than from the examples of his contemporaries, he drew increasingly upon modern masters, as he would for his future sculptures. In *Arts*, R. Warren Dash observed that, with one exception, Segal's works would "not lose their efficacy" if the subject matter was left out.[10] In fact, at this juncture, Segal might have become an abstract

6 artist. Behind his figures, such as those in *The Blow* from 1958, bold bands of color served as grounds that could have worked as pictures in their own right. But Segal was looking for a larger subject, one imbued with deeper meaning, rather than limiting himself, as he saw it, to nonrepresentational canvases. Somehow, he sensed that three-dimensionality would solve the dilemma.

About this time, Segal got hold of some department store mannequins to see how they were fabricated. To his surprise, they were made—in the years before plastic molds became commonplace—from materials not only within his means but already accessible among his farm supplies: plaster and chicken wire. Several years

7. Grace Hartigan
Grand Street Brides, 1954
Oil on canvas, 72 x 102½ in.
Whitney Museum of American Art, New York
Anonymous gift

8. *The Legend of Lot*, 1958
Oil on canvas, 72 x 96 in.; plaster, wood, and chicken-wire figure, height: 72 in.
Collection of the artist

ago, Segal explained why he began to make plaster figures. He said, "In 1958 I was painting six-by-eight-foot canvases with life-size figures on them. They were big, broad, expressionist; full of gesture, full of the means of Abstract Expressionism, which impressed me. Yet I found I couldn't use those means to say what I wanted. That year I built from armature three life-size figures out of plaster—only because I was questioning the realities of space for myself. The way I was taught in painting to refer to space, I felt, severely limited me. There were too many restrictions toward preservation of the flat plane if I was going to paint a 'modern' painting. I felt I had only two alternatives: the illusion of space à la the Renaissance or real space. It became essential for me to try sculpture. Since I had been painting life-size figures, I simply made them life-size out of plaster, but built-up—armature, wire mesh, burlap dipped in plaster."[11]

During February 1959, when Segal next exhibited at the Hansa Gallery, he showed 72-by-96-inch canvases, four of which concerned the biblical story of Lot, his wife, and their daughters. He also included three ungainly life-size figures, made from burlap dipped in plaster and applied over shaped chicken-wire cores. One of these—a standing male nude with a pot belly, crossed arms, and 8 a brooding, truculent manner—was placed in front of a painting

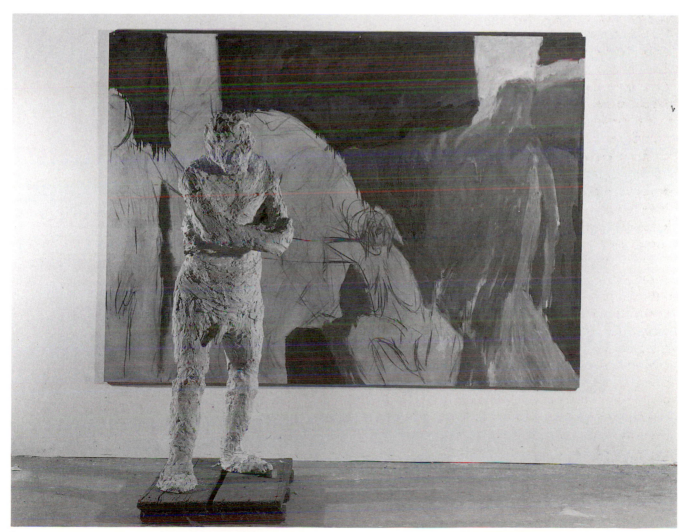

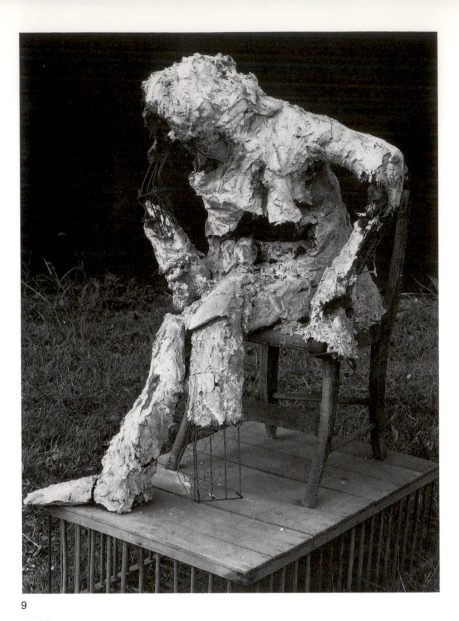

9

with rapidly outlined figures of comparable scale; broad black patches relieved by some red, yellow, and blue passages; and generous amounts of bare canvas. The artist felt that the calcified man looked as if he had stepped out of the picture plane. Today, this is Segal's best-known early work.

The man's two freestanding companions were more independent forms, placed in the center of the room. One was a seated woman; the other, a man sprawled across the ground. They seemed less solid and stoic, moreover, because their wire armatures were visible in several places. The woman slouched in an elegant, period-piece chair with curved legs that contrasted with her disheveled appearance and the old chicken crate that served as a pedestal. The bow-backed man lying, or rather writhing, on the floor, had rather pronounced limbs that made him seem all arms and legs. It was he that was chosen as the illustration for an *Artnews* review and for an early article written on Segal's first cast sculptures. But it was the seated woman who was to have the greatest impact on the artist's future development. What set her apart from her companions were the implications of that actual, manufactured chair. In

9. *Seated Figure*, 1958
Plaster, chicken wire, and wood, 52 x 32 x 36 in.
Collection of the artist

10. *Reclining Woman*, 1958
Plaster and wood, 36 x 78 in.
Collection of the artist

1967 Segal related, "The sharp edges of that real chair really sent me flying, and I began to look at real objects with their hard surfaces, different colors, as plastic [i.e., sculptural] objects. Not props, but rather plastic presences powerful in their own right."[12]

Critics, who had been responding more and more favorably to Segal's paintings, were baffled and uneasy about the sculptures. So was the artist. In the February 1959 *Arts*, the painter and critic Sidney Tillim called the standing man, the sitting woman, and the lying man "outright grotesques."[13] The poet and critic James Schuyler, in that month's *Artnews*, compared the sculptures to "the arrested movement of a Pompeian dog."[14]

During this time, Segal made about a dozen other sculptures, none of which has ever been exhibited. These included several bas-reliefs. One had a reclining odalisque, indebted to Matisse's *Blue Nude* of 1905 for both pose and distorted anatomy. Another relief consisted of a bloated, balloon-limbed earth goddess who could have been a primeval ancestor of Niki de Saint-Phalle's Nanas. A third woman appears naturalistically at ease, with her right knee slightly bent and her right hand placed sassily on her waist. From a distance, her life-size and realistic body make her look not only fully three-dimensional, but also as if she were cast from life. One other figure, a male, was modeled in the round, and placed in a tall wooden cage. The chest of this white sculpture is decorated with bits of thick paint placed like ornamental buttons, and the artist today identifies the container as an elevator.

These four sculptures—the others made during this period no longer exist—incorporate a wealth of ideas and indicate the various approaches Segal suspected he could use if he ceased painting.

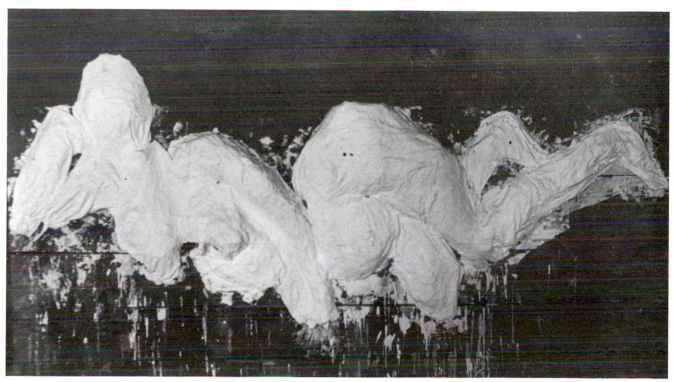

10

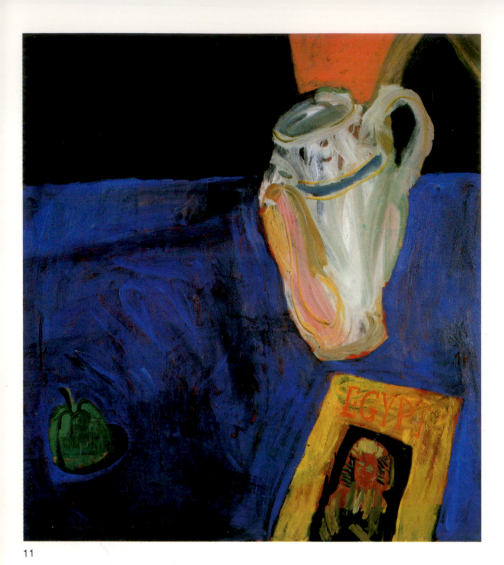

11

Some had rough surfaces; others were smoother. Two were distorted and unnatural; two were astonishingly lifelike. Having hand fashioned plaster forms to achieve particular effects, Segal had only to find a more fruitful method to get what he was after. There were glimmerings of his future course at this point, but he simply did not know how to take the next step. Unhurried, he would be ready to realize the potential of medical bandages when they were introduced to him three years later. For the moment, what he had created would remain dormant.

In the meantime, Segal continued to paint. He even included canvases along with sculptures in his M.A. thesis exhibition held at Douglass College, Rutgers's sister school, in January 1963, a year and a half after he had begun casting from life. The modern masters still intrigued him, but now he went back to the source rather than relying upon those who had been its heirs. Matisse, particularly the Matisse of *Bathers by the River*, was frequently evoked in matters of scale and size, figuration and background. As Segal established his own style, his random borrowings from the greats of modernism became less readily apparent.

13   A case in point is *Red Courbet*, a garish canvas exhibited in November–December 1960 in his first show at the newly opened Green Gallery, directed by Richard Bellamy (the Hansa had closed

11.   *Egyptian Still Life*, c. 1960
Oil on canvas, 36 x 40 in.
Roy and Dorothy Lichtenstein

12.   George Segal painting, June 1960

13.   *Red Courbet*, 1959
Oil on canvas, 72 x 96 in.
Collection of the artist

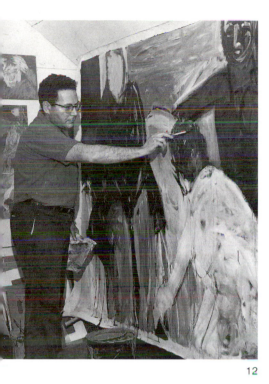

at the end of the 1958–59 art season). Two fleshy women with swelling thighs lie on a bed indicated only by broad passages of paint. The ecstatically embracing pair is accompanied by a blue male. Details are avoided in favor of gesture and pose. Outlines are pronounced; contrasts are harsh. Color is bold. Even though this painting fits right in with Segal's other canvases from this period, it is indebted to Courbet's *Sleep* of 1866, which Segal saw at the Courbet exhibition held during the spring of 1960 at the Philadelphia Museum of Art.

Of all the masters of art history, it is Courbet who painted the body types that one most readily associates with Segal's oeuvre (Rubens too comes to mind). Yet, in his homage, Segal made one significant change. Rather than representing two female lovers as the Frenchman had done, he depicted a menage à trois. And, while the general outlines of the scene are indebted to Courbet's *Sleep*, the background, as in many of Segal's other contemporary paintings, has qualities in common with the abstractions of both Barnett Newman and Mark Rothko. To span formally the gulf between past and present, between art historical sources and present-day practices still remains a central concern for Segal.

12

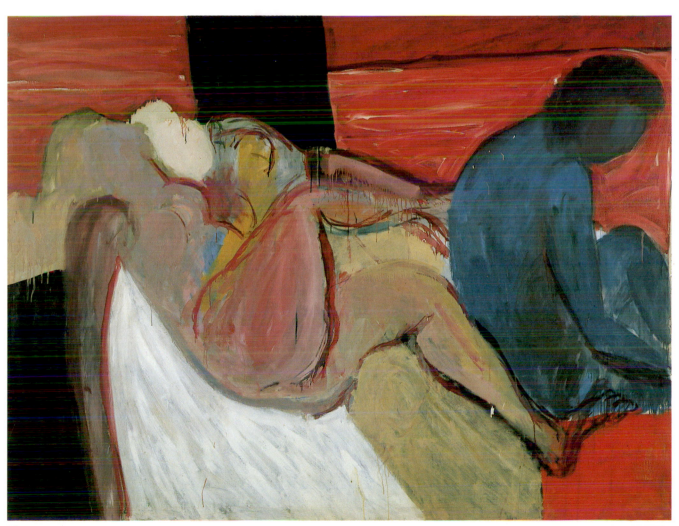

13

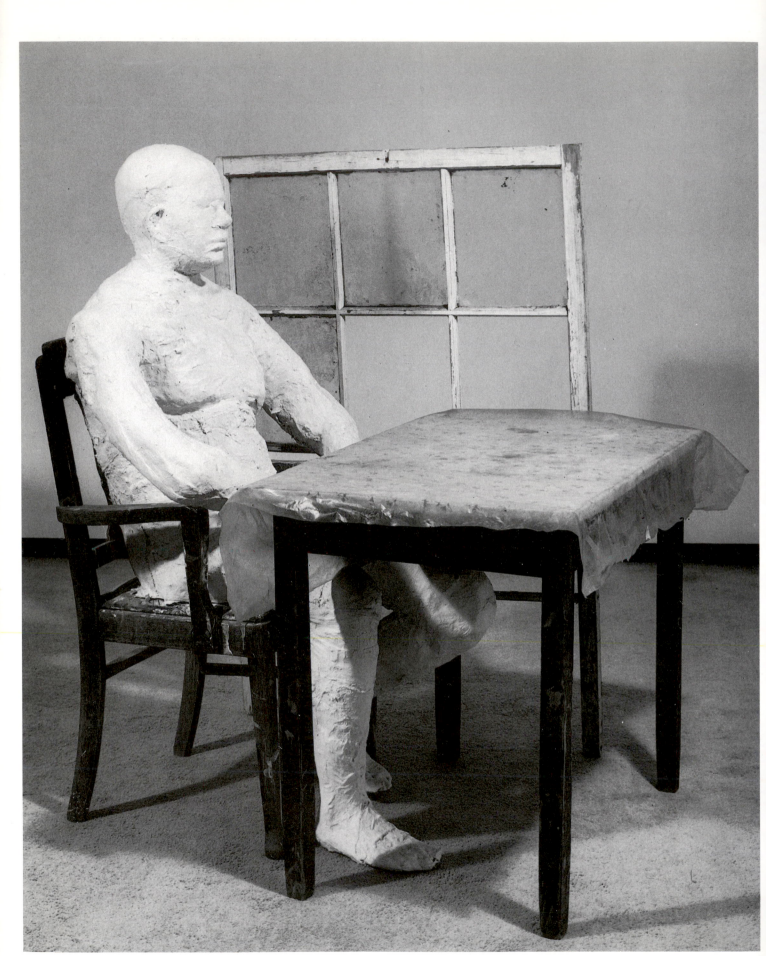

14

2 Early Cast Sculpture

In July 1961 a student who was the wife of a chemist at the nearby Johnson and Johnson laboratories brought to one of Segal's classes some recently perfected medical bandages, cloth strips that would facilitate the setting of broken bones. This discovery propelled her instructor into the phase of his career that has brought him world fame. At that moment, George Segal became a sculptor. Previously, he had been a painter who had made some sculptures. Now, for a short while, he would be a sculptor who also made paintings.

"Immediately, I knew what I wanted to do," Segal told a *Newsweek* reporter in 1965, recalling that epiphany. He explained further: "I was my own first model. I wrapped myself in the bandages and my wife put on the plaster. I had a hell of a time getting the pieces off and reassembled. But it eventually became *Man at a Table*. I had found my medium."[15]

The handmade sculptures from 1958 had been, in Segal's words, "rough, unfinished, emphasizing only gesture and bulk." He had not continued in this vein because, he would later say, "I wanted more definition." By wrapping bandages around live models, hitherto not an accepted artistic practice, Segal could capture scores of details. Pliable ⅛-inch-thick molds pick up precise records of clothing and anatomy. But Segal was not yet interested in specific bits of information—a frayed shirt sleeve, a missing button, the pockmarks of a face. For the moment, the white, cakey exteriors provided him with all that he was after—just the right amount of substance in terms of body weight and pose to bridge the gap between the sketchy figures he had outlined in his paintings and the spatial definition he sought by working in three dimensions. Presence was asserted. Feelings were evoked. Segal was not trying to replicate reality. Rather, he was at last able to achieve an art that united representation, formal attributes, and philosophical meaning.

For the most part, the critical literature merely notes the fact that Segal grasped the moment to wrap himself in gauze bandages that his wife, newly recruited as a studio assistant, then slathered with plaster. For the artist, however, the situation was pregnant with a host of implications. He had already mastered the art of rendering a human form on canvas, but owing to the strictures of

14

14. *Man at a Table*, 1961
Plaster, wood, and glass, 53 x 48 x 48 in.
Städtisches Museum Abteiberg
Mönchengladbach, West Germany

23

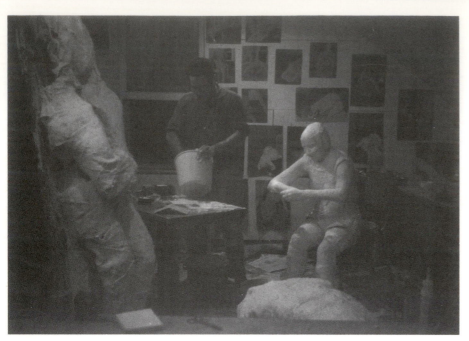

15

modernism, he had been denied the chance to produce a convincing context for his figures. It should therefore not be overlooked that in his first cast sculpture, Segal sat himself down on an old chair, beside a dirty window, and in front of a table covered with a soiled plastic cloth. "I was fascinated," the artist mentioned in 1967, "by the plastic [i.e., sculptural] play of the innumerable legs."[16]

Henceforth Segal would locate his figures in environments. The meanings in his evocative world derive almost always from this integration of plaster figures with real components. A bus driver steers a wheel that came from a discarded public vehicle. A taxi fleet owner leans wearily against a door from a 1956 Mercury sedan. A woman stands vacantly in the doorway of a tenement. With Segal's new means, background had become as prominent as foreground. Everyday artifacts have the import of cast forms. The space around the leg of a table is coequal to the space around the leg of a human model. The colors of carefully selected objects contrast with the figures' white surfaces.

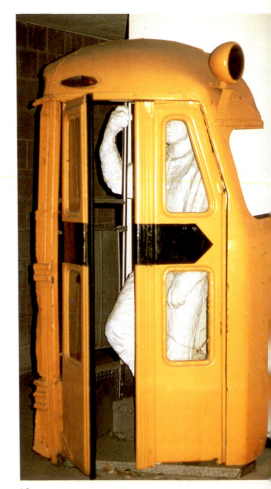

In 1965 Segal said, "I remember my life with objects and I also look at these objects 'plastically' (I suppose that is the term), 'esthetically,' for what these shapes are. And how people relate to these shapes and how they don't relate in a human way intrigues me."[17] A year later, he added, "And isn't it amazing, if you take seven different people, or ten different people or four hundred different people, they won't choose the same objects. And if you collect enough objects selected by one person, they are going to be uncanny in that they represent an insight into the vision that the person has of the world."[18]

The situations staged by Segal suggest the dreams of a philosopher. The art historian Charles Mitchell compares this aspect of the artist's sculptures to the kind of "magic of the streets" created by Giorgio de Chirico. Segal's ghostly, catatonic figures put the viewer at a distance. They are like us, and yet they are not of

16

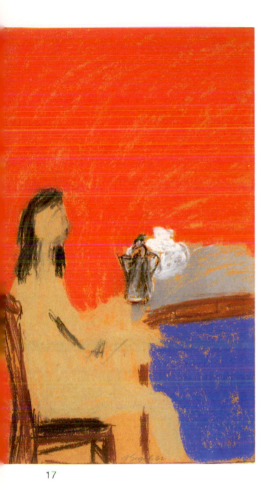

17

15. George Segal mixing plaster, November 1961

16. *Man Leaving a Bus*, 1967
Plaster, metal, and glass, 88½ x 39 x 33½ in.
Private collection

17. Untitled, 1962
Pastel on paper, 18 x 12 in.
Private collection

our world. The objects that define task and occupations, however, attract closer scrutiny because these props help structure the viewer's own life. Thus, at the same time that one is perceiving imaginary characters, one might also feel impelled to sit down on a vacant stool in *The Diner* or patiently wait one's turn to play the pinball machine in *Gottlieb's Wishing Well*. A feeling is evoked, then, of being an unexpected guest at a hallucinatory event in ordinary life.

There are times when Segal environments eerily suggest episodes from the old television show *The Twilight Zone*. One of these programs comes readily to mind: a department store customer rode on an elevator to a floor not indicated on the control panel, and found himself surrounded by mannequins acting out the roles for which they were dressed. Rather than passively watching, a visitor to a Segal exhibition is drawn in to become an uneasy participant. We know and have used these objects, but how our bodies have been transformed!

Achieving what he was after involved more than Segal's covering a seated model with bandages and plaster. *Man at a Table* was begun during July 1961. During the next five months, only two other sculptures—*Woman in a Restaurant Booth* and *Woman Painting Her Fingernails*—were made. Segal had found his technique, but he had not yet established all of the concepts he hoped to embody in his environments. That took a bit of deliberation.

A number of decisions had to be made. For example, before Segal executed his second sculpture, he had at least three requirements: the person to be cast "had to be a figure I knew well, either a close friend or a relative"; that person furthermore had to be situated "in a familiar place, with real furniture"; and the artist had to leave for himself "a place to sit down."

While he was grappling with the overall physical design and philosophical character of the sculptures, Segal continued to paint and to produce pastels. Not surprisingly, his canvases from this year are filled with figures in extravagant poses that could never be obtained in three dimensions. Reviewing an exhibition the artist held at the Green Gallery during the spring of 1962—a show in which pastels, paintings, and sculptures were all featured—Jill Johnston, in *Artnews*, noted how the pictures contained "Figures in various bending, lying, sitting 'gestures' [which] are not so stable as their size and weight would have them be if they were not a part of a total sweeping action of paint. . . ."[19] Not yet having accepted his vocation as a sculptor, Segal found his pictorial efforts entering a state of crisis that at last he could resolve only by working in three dimensions.

It was while preparing for this show that Segal also encountered a problem that had not been as evident when hanging canvases: the three-dimensional works had to be lit. In 1972 Segal recalled, "One of the first times that I was setting up sculpture, I found myself on a ladder jiggling the lights in the ordinary fashion of a gallery director, and I discovered that every time I shifted the lights the meaning of my sculpture changed."[20] Because of this experience, the sculptor today tries to supervise every major presentation of his art. Success has changed the life of George Segal very little, with the one exception that he has traveled all over the world to help install his works.

Most of Segal's initial sculptures have seated figures; tables and chairs thus operate as formal design elements, as interesting shapes, and as objects informed by their owner's taste. Unmatched pieces 19 of furniture, for example, appear in *The Dinner Table*. They add visual variety and reveal something about either the homeowners' lack of formality or their penchant for yard-sales. Like *The Dinner* 18 *Table*, other early works such as *The Bus Driver* (1962) and *Man on a Bicycle* (1962) incorporated round forms as part of the over-all design. Segal's new art was so startling when it first appeared, and people so often take for granted the look of objects they daily encounter, that the formal play of multiple legs and the use of wheels in these early pieces has rarely, if ever, been commented upon. But, for the artist, these were important matters.

The Dinner Table, *Lovers on a Bench*, *Lovers on a Bed*, and *The* 21 *Bus Riders*—four sculptures from 1962—include a number of figures. A total of nineteen men and women appear in the first nine three-dimensional works Segal executed. (One hundred are among his first sixty-nine.) His canvases had frequently had triadic groups of characters. Having become comfortable with relating figures to one another in his paintings, the artist continued his practice in

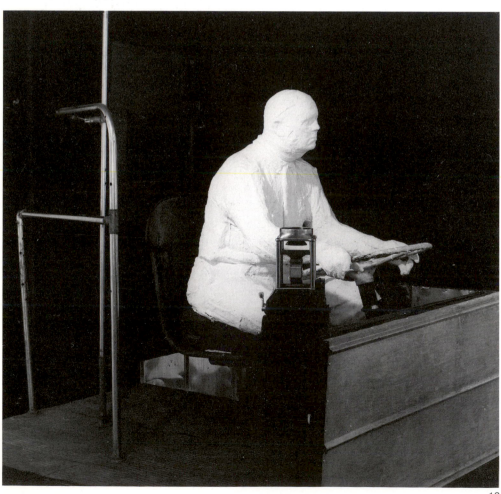

18

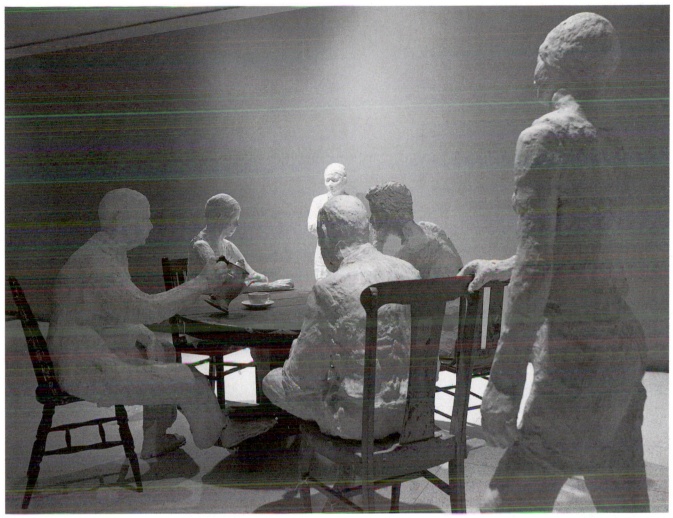

19

his sculptures. Consequently, his mature art encompasses more freestanding parts than one generally finds in twentieth-century sculpture.

All of the early sculptures explore different ideas. *The Dinner Table*, the fifth sculpture Segal made, remains one of his most ambitious in its use of four seated and two standing figures and in its unusually large size (72 by 120 by 120 inches). Segal said in January 1963, "All the figures around the table are people I know very well. . . . I'm holding the coffee pot. The figure off against the wall is my wife. All the personal relationships and tension of those particular people with each other, I tried to put into this piece."[21] But the psychological complexity of *The Dinner Table* was just one facet of its overall design. The artist was also concerned with another goal—achieving meaningful spatial relationships. The "negative" spaces are as consciously dealt with as the "positive" forms. The two interlock. Segal practically carves the atmosphere that surrounds his figures. Because the molds are pliable and can be reshaped, the space between crossed legs, for example, can be carefully contoured. In March 1964 the artist said, "I put figures and objects into a space, and then invite you to

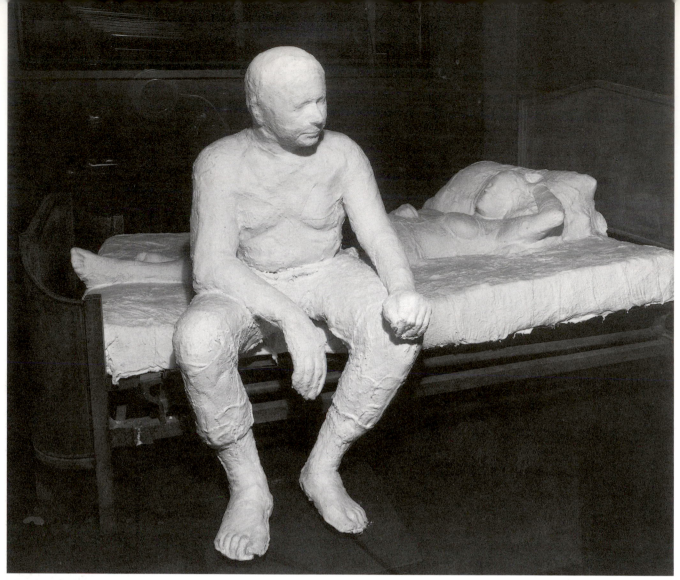

20

walk within that space and encounter these figures in many different relationships."[22]

Early on, Segal seems to have meticulously studied how he could incorporate a host of formal devices with thought-provoking content. (When she was seven, Segal's daughter would occasionally inform a telephone caller that her father was busy "thinking.") In *Lovers on a Bed*, Segal consciously used the entwined bodies of his lovers as a vehicle for formal concerns as much as a focus of emotional interest. Arms and legs can be viewed as impersonally as fallen tree trunks with gnarled branches, while the headboard frames the bodies like a painted mandorla.

The Bus Riders, Segal's next composition with several individuals, and the ninth sculpture he cast, reveals yet another of his concerns: contemporary political events. At the time *The Bus Riders* was executed, the issue of riding in the back of the bus in the Deep South was constantly in the headlines. Three seated figures and a standing passenger ride grimly off to some distant destination. One figure has nodded off; another daydreams. Formally, the tall man anchors the scene with his pronounced vertical torso. In terms of viewer participation, a space has been left for

20. *Couple on a Bed*, 1965
Plaster and metal, 47 x 81 x 50 in.
The Art Institute of Chicago
Gift of Mr. and Mrs. Robert B. Mayer

21. *The Bus Riders*, 1962
Plaster, metal, and vinyl, 69 x 40 x 76 in.
Hirshhorn Museum and Sculpture Garden,
Smithsonian Institution, Washington, D.C.

one other person to sit down among the three shadowy travelers.

Segal's work of the 1960s is populated by stocky bodies. Initially, the artist did not purposefully seek out people with large frames. Rather, he found his own size reflected among the friends and relatives he asked to pose. Nevertheless, such builds have contributed immeasurably to the monumental character of his art. Because Segal was not originally interested in emphasizing detail, his choice of heavyset people made additional sense. When cast, ample girths could support on their plaster shells rough, smudgy puddles that enhanced the expressionist character of the works. Slender physiques presented themselves as appropriate models only when the artist altered his casting procedures in the early 1970s and sought more anatomical definition. Thus, form and technique intertwine in his sculpture.

21

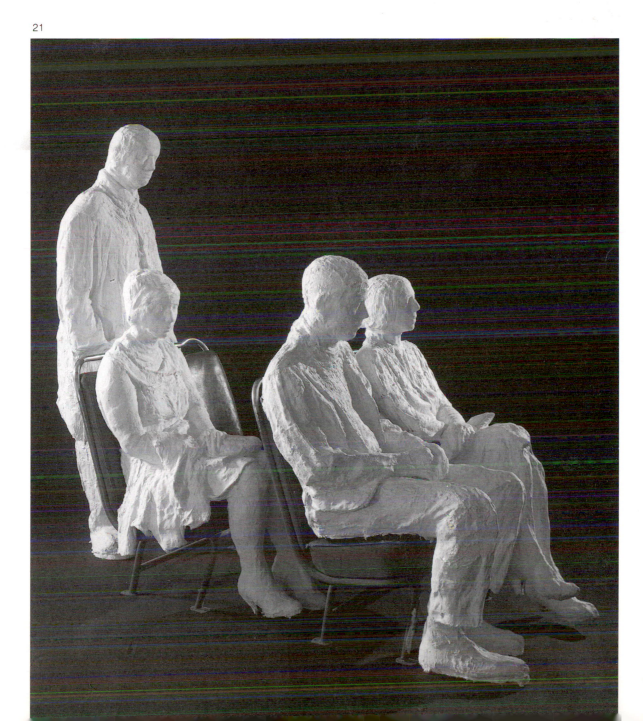

In September 1962 Segal enrolled in the Masters degree program at Rutgers University, still believing that he could not make a living from his art and that he would have to teach college in order to support his family. Rutgers, at that moment, was as special as N.Y.U. had been in the years following World War II. The New Brunswick campus nurtured so many artists during this period that the Bianchini Gallery in 1965 mounted *Ten from Rutgers University*, a sampling of the artists who were part of that scene.[23] With an extraordinary potpourri of interests, these men availed themselves of the advantages of interdisciplinary activities and incorporated into their endeavors a particular intellectual flavor. Recalling their joint adventures, Kaprow later wrote, "The best artists do not come from art, and the best art comes from the least expected place."[24]

Ironically, within two months of his becoming a student again, Segal's sculptures suddenly became widely known when they were associated with a new art movement. His work and that by Roy Lichtenstein, Claes Oldenburg, Jim Dine, Andy Warhol, James Rosenquist, Robert Indiana, and Tom Wesselmann drew national attention after being included in *The New Realists*, an exhibition organized by the Sidney Janis Gallery in 1962. The media adopted another name for what was displayed in this landmark show, and it stuck: Pop art. This new wave of American painters and sculptors toppled the hegemony of Abstract Expressionism. The public responded readily to the recognizable images, bright colors, and abstract accents embodied in their art.

Home and highway, supermarket shelves, and the pages of the daily news provided these artists with countless visual motifs and iconographic themes. Commercial techniques and mundane materials also offered new possibilities. Lichtenstein, for example, fashioned his images with fields of benday dots. Rosenquist exploited skills he had developed as a billboard painter. Oldenburg and Segal made their sculptures with humble plaster instead of powerful steel or elegant marble.

These new images and techniques were nonetheless wedded to the principles of abstraction. In her first published article, Barbara Rose cogently pointed out, ". . . it is now obvious there exists a group of artists who have chosen the middle way out of Abstract Expressionism (the path between a kind of simplified abstract image and new figure painting)."[25] As each artist refined his own visual language, the debt of this new movement to previous nonrepresentational art was obscured and subsequently overlooked.

Years later Segal would say, "What's called Pop art is a clustering of very different individuals. And, after the public excitement dies down, each man is always thrust on his own resources."[26]

Segal and his wife sailed to Europe for his October 1963 show at the Galerie Ileana Sonnabend in Paris. (Nine cast figures shared the couple's stateroom.) One night the Segals and Sonnabends saw a *son et lumière* display in the formal gardens of Versailles. Not long ago, Michael Sonnabend remembered how, when the spotlights beamed across the carved marbles, all were struck by the way their stark, dramatic whiteness resembled a gallery filled with Segal's art. The geometric organization of the gardens also made

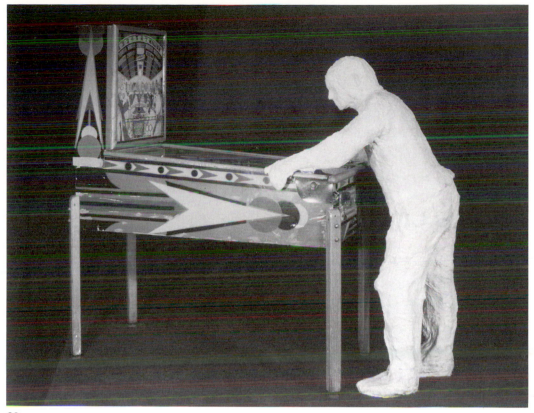

22

an impression on them. The next day, Segal was ready to make a sculpture inspired by the previous evening's experiences. He asked Michael Sonnabend if a pinball machine could be procured. It could, and Sonnabend became the figure operating the flippers in *Gottlieb's Wishing Well*, a title that makes an ironic reference to the Abstract Expressionist paintings of Adolph Gottlieb. Reminiscing about the incident that gave birth to this sculpture, Sonnabend noted that the patterning of the pinball machine reminded him of the Cartesian layout of the grounds of Versailles. For Sonnabend, *Gottlieb's Wishing Well* draws together "*son et lumière*, Descartes, and classical gardens." Segal, he says, "doesn't want to freeze the world. He wants to externalize situations."

Upon returning to America, Segal supervised the installation of *Cinema* in the *Four Environments* exhibition at the Sidney Janis Gallery in February 1964 and readied work for a one-man show at the Green Gallery that March. One of Segal's most riveting sculptures, *Cinema* manages to be both ethereal and bold.[27] Its luminous quality casts a wonderful glow. Its red letters create a commanding presence. The subject of *Cinema* is familiar; its principles of composition, abstract. A large man stretches toward a capital *R* mounted on a backlit marquee. The figure was cast by the sculptor; everything else was either purchased or made by the artist. In highfalutin' terms, one might call Segal a Renaissance man; certainly he is a jack-of-all-trades. In the old days a painter or a sculptor purchased supplies at an art store. During the 1960s someone like Segal bought materials like those in *Cinema*—metal, plexiglass, and fluorescent light—at a local hardware shop.

In 1967, responding to a survey about the "Sensibility of the

22. *Gottlieb's Wishing Well*, 1963
Plaster and pinball machine, 65 x 25 x 76 in.
Private collection

Sixties," Segal wrote, "The sensibility of the sixties is characterized by an openness of attitude, a willingness to use unfamiliar materials, forms and unorthodox stances in the work produced, an unwillingness to accept standard value judgments, a tendency to probe, act, live, and work with final judgment suspended, an appreciation of the mystery, unknowability, ambiguity of the simplest things."[28] *Cinema* is such a mixture of formal invention and psychological representation.

Segal is curious about people—what they do, how they act. He is, by nature, an observer. "I'm interested in their gestures and I'm interested in their experiences and mine," he has said.[29] "In the early days," he once noted, "I spent a lot of time trying to look as bluntly as I could at people in their environments. Very often I saw them against garish light, illuminated signs. I saw them against visually vivid objects that were considered low class, anti-art, un-art, kitsch, disreputable, and I suppose [*Cinema*] is like some of those attitudes of that time."

Cinema is a white abstraction. Its gridlike organization and sly use of black and red evoke Mondrian. And, as in an Analytic Cubist painting, the letters function as design elements, as signifiers of identity, and as contributors of color. The work also shares an affinity with the artist's earlier canvases. The man has the bulk of Segal's painted figures, and with the piece lit from behind, a viewer is made aware of the differentiation between foreground and background. The gesture of the figure echoes that of a character in *The Blow*, a painting from the late 1950s.

The tale of *Cinema*'s inception vividly illustrates how quickly Segal glimpses and grasps what he wants to use in his art. The sculptor has related how, at two o'clock one morning, driving home from a visit to New York, he noticed "a fellow reaching up to pluck off the last letter from an illuminated sign." Seconds later, after he told his wife to look, the moment had passed. Segal has noted that he was interested in the formal qualities of the scene, but he nevertheless felt that he was merely recreating something espied from a moving vehicle. Yet he discovered that he was mistaken, for he had actually interpreted something he *thought* he had seen. "After I finished building the piece I drove down in the daytime to the real sign. It was built differently from the way I perceived it."

Segal self-effacingly claims, "I get a flash in my head and then I have to go into my studio, under a controlled situation, like a carpenter, like a construction worker, and reconstruct a physical, tangible image of something that's in my head." In the studio, though, he becomes an artist rather than a witness. A wealth of experience and emotions affects our interpretations of daily life. George Segal transforms such things into art.

George Segal's fame as a sculptor has colored perception of how *Cinema* figures in his oeuvre. When the artist incorporated lights into his later environments, *Cinema* emerged as a prototype; the fact that it was also an outgrowth of earlier canvases receded into the shadows. The shimmering wall of white light, flat and planar, is a pictorial device transformed into sculptural language. The plastic marquee is an abstract background, a feature that critics

23. *Cinema*, 1963
Plaster, metal, plexiglass, and fluorescent light,
118 x 96 x 39 in.
Albright-Knox Art Gallery, Buffalo, New York
Gift of Seymour H. Knox, 1964

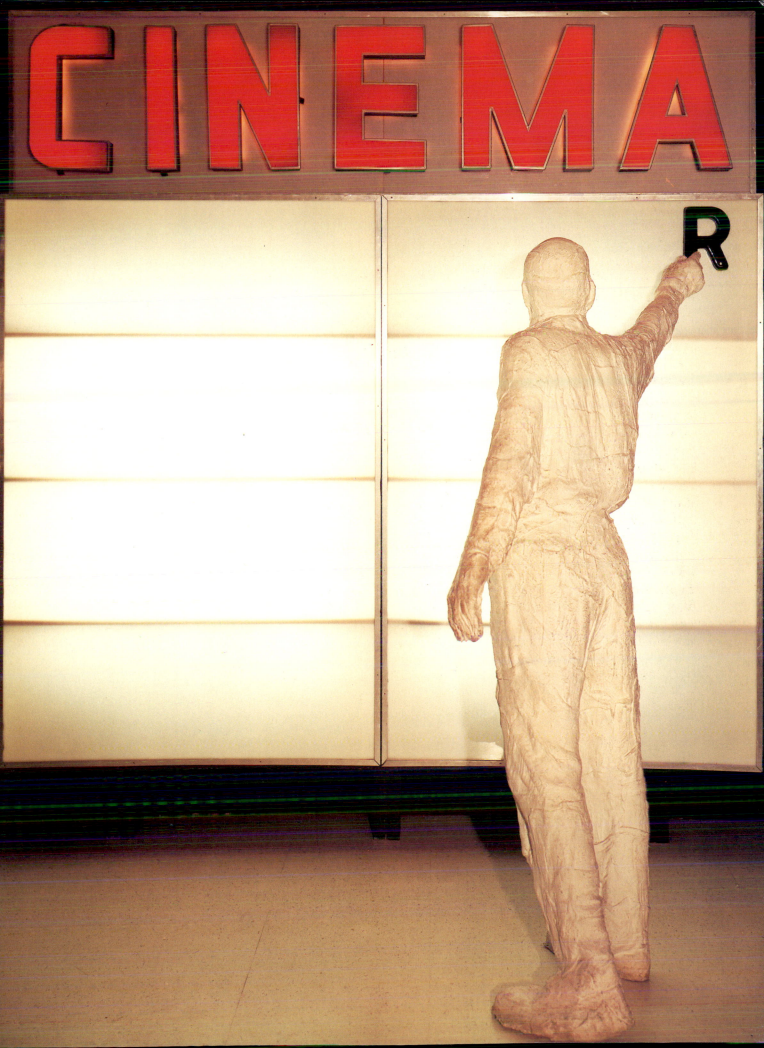

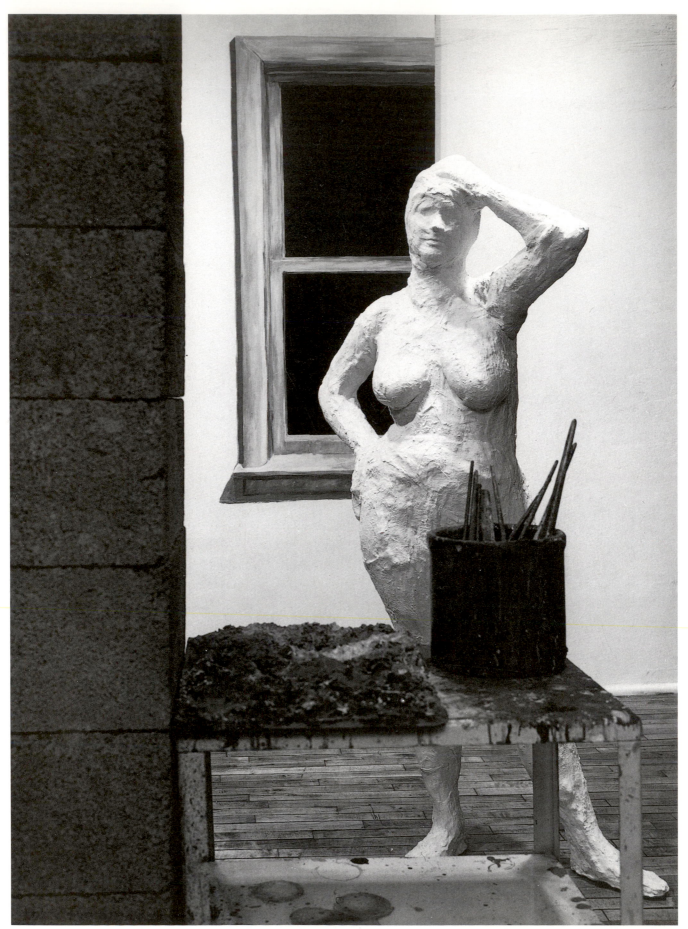

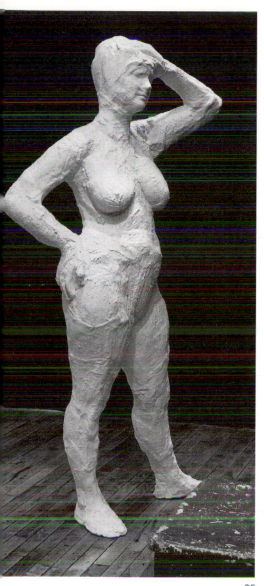

25

had praised in Segal's exhibitions at the Hansa Gallery. And in *Cinema*, the sign-changer is as close to the rear surface of the work as a three-dimensional figure can be without becoming a relief. Thus, Segal succinctly accomplished in three dimensions what he had previously sought to create on canvas: the rendition of a rotund figure against a flat, abstract ground.

In 1963 Segal was still very much engaged with the problem of combining aspects of picture making with sculptural space. This is tellingly revealed in *The Artist's Studio*, executed on the heels of 24 *Cinema*. Rather than relying on a drawing (something Segal rarely does, although he has made hundreds of pastels over the years), he adapted the environment from a painting type of the late 1950s. Its theme, which had served as the basis for many canvases he showed at the Hansa Gallery, was inspired by the intimate studio scenes with models by Edgar Degas, Pierre Bonnard, and Henri Matisse (one striking predecessor for this kind of Segal is the Fauve's *Standing Nude* of 1901).

Space is a crucial formal component in *The Artist's Studio*, and it is defined in a way that was to influence the work that followed. Atmosphere is almost more palpable than the props and quite as intriguing as the model. The front and back planes are clearly bounded; the sides are not. A viewer is aware of entering this scene and moving about in its free-flowing space. After *The Artist's Studio* was completed, Segal said, "The air between the objects, its density, is just as much a part of the whole as the solid objects."[30] That is certainly true in this pivotal sculpture.

The Artist's Studio, along with *Cinema*, marks the end of one phase of Segal's career and the start of another. In both sculptures, the artist resolved in three dimensions formal ideas that he had not been able to realize fully in his paintings. Even when Segal's later works have a frontal, planar composition, they are less pictorial than what had come before. Space had been conquered, and henceforth it would have a sculptural quality in his oeuvre.

24. *The Artist's Studio*, 1963
Plaster, wood, metal, paint, and mixed media,
96 x 72 x 108 in.
Private collection

25. *The Artist's Studio*, detail

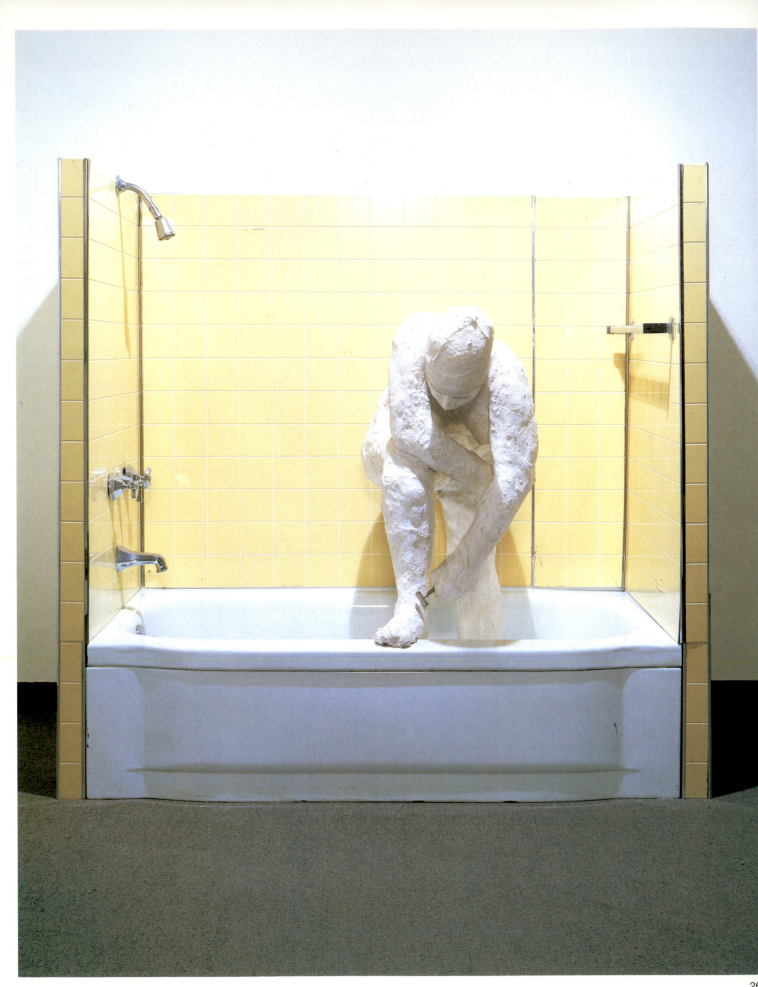

3 Theme and Variation

By the time he had made fourteen sculptures, George Segal had explored a variety of approaches to formal properties, subject matter, and content upon which he would build in future works. At times, one component might overshadow the other two; often the mixture would be more equally balanced. Theme and variation, a concept evident in his paintings, was to play an ever larger role as his range of subjects became broader. *The Artist's Studio* spawned numerous compositions of nude women, many in settings defined merely by the inclusion of a single chair. *Cinema* generated several environments based on small businesses. A score of lovers were cast from life in various situations and states of dress or undress. Several works dealt with modern art and how it has been made.

In *Woman Shaving Her Leg* (1963) pose and space illustrate how Segal developed variations on the theme of the nude model. He uses body language to communicate form and meaning forcefully. Unlike the placement of the model in *The Artist's Studio*, the stance of this woman is less self-conscious because it is integral to the task at hand. Although the gesture of her arms is significant, it is her whole body—the way her back is bent, for example—that carries the weight of the sculpture. *Woman Shaving Her Leg*, which incorporates a re-creation of the artist's own tub-shower, has a frontal viewpoint. A subtle inflection governs this space; it could be simply pictorial, but instead it has an unexpected three-dimensional presence.

Because Segal has always been interested in psychological, philosophical, and political issues, it seems appropriate that when he made *Woman Shaving Her Leg*, he chose a subject that was soon to become a topic of concern for the Women's Movement (as would *Woman Buckling Her Bra*, also of 1963). When Segal makes art from what he sees around him, he often chances upon mundane images with a deeper significance that others may not notice. The artist balances his detailed view of the everyday world with an awareness of broader relevance. Social scientists study facts and figures. Segal keeps his eyes open.

Having enveloped the women in *The Artist's Studio* and *Woman Shaving Her Leg* in two different kinds of space, Segal discarded

26. *Woman Shaving Her Leg*, 1963
Plaster, metal, porcelain, and Masonite
63 x 65 x 30 in.
Mrs. Robert B. Mayer
On long-term loan to the Museum of
Contemporary Art, Chicago

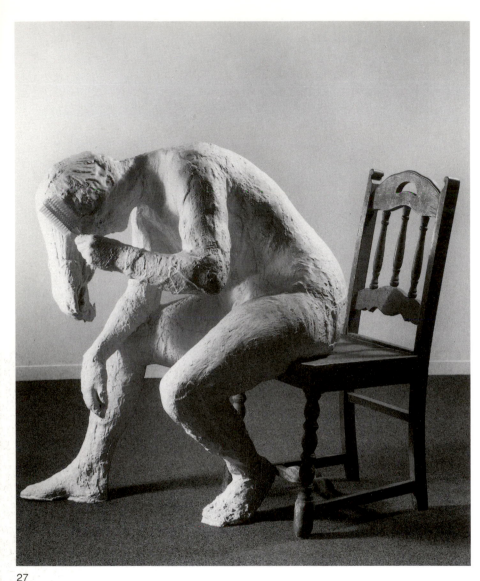

27

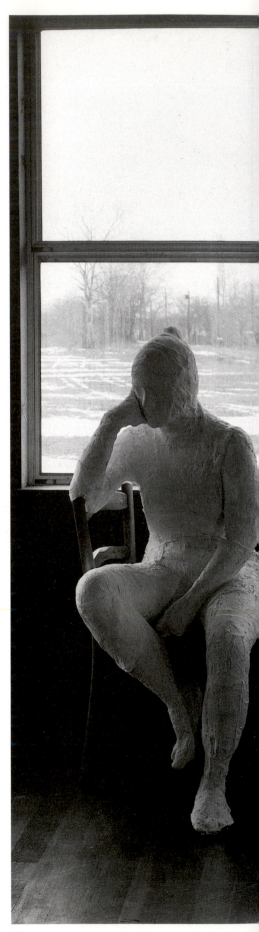

the use of environments altogether when working with nudes. During the next several years, he seated a number of models in chairs and executed no-environment environments. In such toilette scenes as *Woman Brushing Her Hair* (1965), *Seated Woman* (1967), *Woman Putting Up Her Hair* (1967), and *Woman Putting On Her Shoe* (1968), the stark white plaster figures contrast with the colors of the objects. Segal's nudes are humble women. Their bodies are not the sort celebrated in calendars tacked to gas station walls. They are not even the fresh-faced girl next door. These are the wives and sisters to whom the gas station attendants and factory workers return home every night. Had they been cast standing, these robust ladies might have looked like traditional statues. But given their self-absorption in banal activities, they could never be mistaken as members of the "marmorean flock" that populated nineteenth-century American sculpture.

   As viewers, we gaze at these fleshy nudes as if we belonged in a painting of Susanna and the Elders. Because there seems to be so little to see in comparison to other sculptures by Segal, we focus on

27, 28
29, 30

28

the way the artist has carved the space between arms and legs. In his pastels (which are almost invariably of women), Segal concentrates on gesture; in his sculptures with similar models, he is able to incorporate clues to the subject's character, because body language and facial expressions are more assertive in three dimensions.

In *Woman Listening to Music* (1965), a nude, her back to the viewer, lies beside a shelf supporting hi-fi equipment. Vivaldi's *Beatus Vir* (Psalm 112, which begins, "Blessed is a man that feareth the Lord, that delighteth in his commandments . . . ") blares forth its transcendent chords from the turntable. The inclusion of sound reflects the influence of Happenings upon the sculptor. However, Segal modified the strident nature of Kaprow's invention to his own means by using great music to elevate this environment to an exalted plateau.

Multiple themes weave their way through Segal's work, and he has often developed several different ones at the same time. While

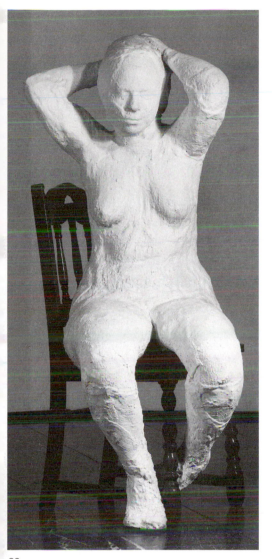

29

27. *Woman Brushing Her Hair*, 1965
Plaster, wood, and plastic, 40 x 24 x 46 in.
Private collection

28. *Seated Woman*, 1967
Plaster and wood, 52 x 42 x 16 in.
Private collection

29. *Woman Putting Up Her Hair*, 1967
Plaster and wood, 53 x 24 x 26 in.
Neue Galerie, Aachen
Ludwig Collection

30. *Woman Putting On Her Shoe*, 1968
Plaster, wood, and plastic, 37 x 24 x 48 in.
William S. Paley

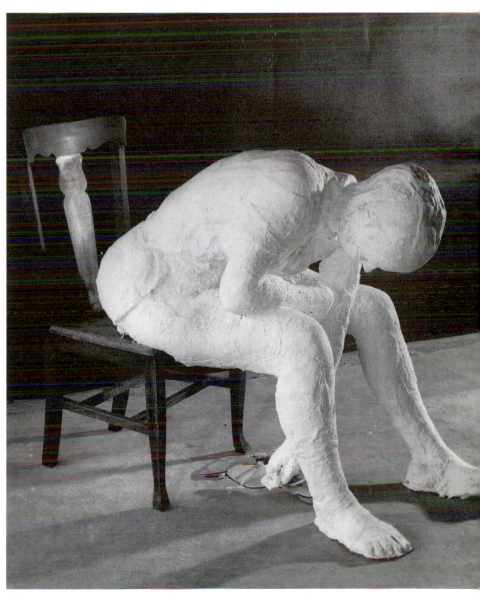

30

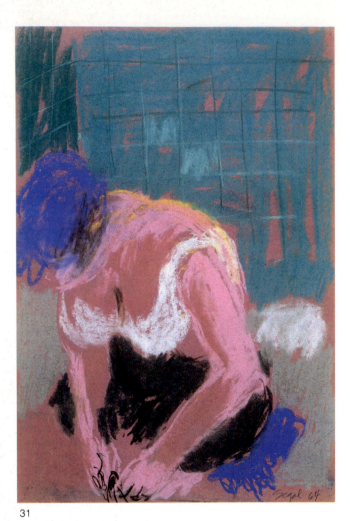

31

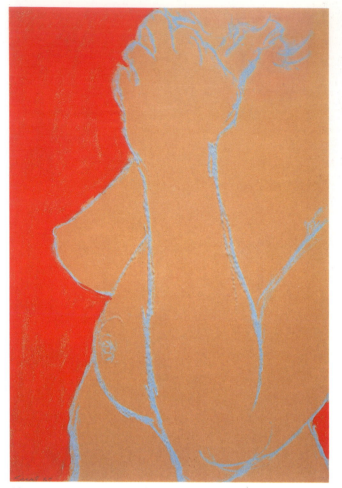

32

making the nude models influenced by *The Artist's Studio*, Segal also produced a category of works descended from *Cinema*: small enterprises or mom-and-pop stores. This group includes *The Gas Station* (1964), *The Dry-Cleaning Store* (1964), *The Butcher Shop* (1965), and *The Diner* (1964–66). The roots of these works go back to the years the artist lived in the Bronx, but they were also nourished by his experiences as an adult in and around New Brunswick and by the highway culture of New Jersey. Until a few years ago, a visitor to Segal's home used as a landmark a Gulf station like the one in his sculpture. Another environment used a New Brunswick dry-cleaning store as a model. *The Butcher Shop* is a loving re-creation of the store Segal's father ran near the Concourse during the 1930s and '40s. *The Diner* resembles an allnight eatery where Segal would stop for a cup of coffee after an evening in Manhattan. Though each environment expresses deep personal meaning, the scenes are general enough that they could take place in Williamstown, Massachusetts, or Davenport, Iowa. For many people, these are the works most identified with the name George Segal.

Segal completed *The Gas Station* just before the opening of his one-person show at the Green Gallery in the spring of 1964. Begun before he had gone to Europe the previous autumn, it was finished

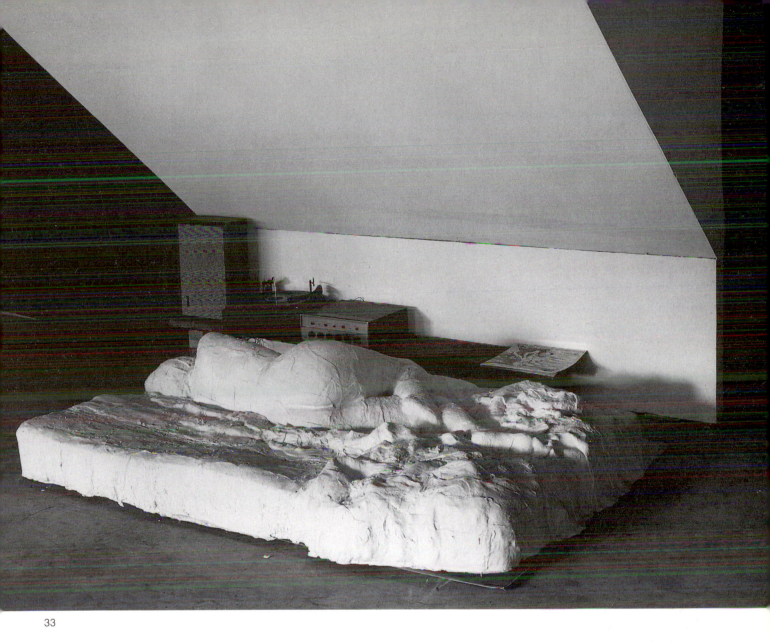

33

after his return to the States, much influenced by his visit abroad.

The Gas Station is 24 feet long, 8 feet high, and 5 feet deep. In its lateral spread, it is an example of what Pontus Hulten has characterized as "American space," which differs from Renaissance space and Cubist space. On the left, behind two plate-glass windows whose metal rims function like an immense picture frame enclosing a color-field painting, a mechanic works among a pyramid of red oil containers; a shelf with another series of red, white, and blue cans; and a row of seven black tires. A lone tire propped against a corner adds a circular accent to this linear design. A wide, pregnant space spanning the middle of the filling station is interrupted only by a ticking Bulova wall clock. On the right, a tired attendant slouches wearily upon an upended crate between three boxes filled with empties and an old-fashioned red Coca-Cola dispenser. This compositional order calls to mind both Simone Martini's *Annunciation* of 1333 and Morris Louis's Unfurled canvases of 1960, in which depicted forms anchor the ends of paintings with vast, empty centers.

31. *Series IV, 1964–3*, 1964
Pastel on paper, 18 x 12 in.
Courtesy the Art Museum and Galleries,
California State University, Long Beach

32. *Untitled*, 1965
Pastel on paper, 18 x 12 in.
Phyllis Tuchman

33. *Woman Listening to Music*, 1965
Plaster, wood, and hi fi set, 72 x 96 x 72 in.
Spencer A. Samuels, New York

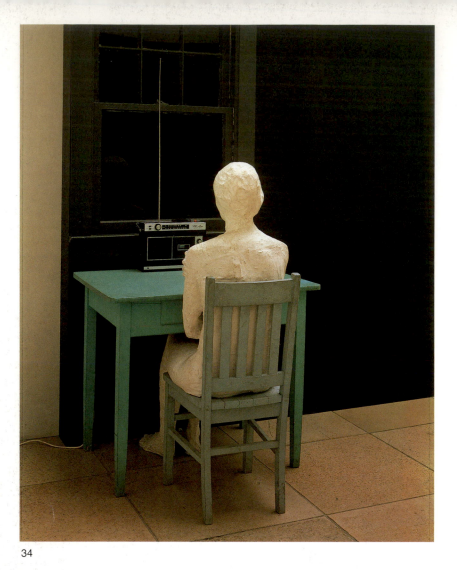

34

The formal unities of *The Gas Station* belong to the principles of classic abstraction and foreshadow, by a year, the emerging Minimalist style: few but bright colors, crisp boundaries, lateral spread, and theatrical space. Into this compositional mixture, however, Segal introduces the content of figuration. We recognize these individuals and this place. Gas stations play special roles in American life. The *New York Times* once published a feature on Raineri's service station in Passaic, New Jersey, because local politicians fraternize there every Sunday morning. In her short story *The Ocean*, Bobbie Ann Mason captured the mythic dimensions that Billy Carter's pumps in Plains, Georgia, once assumed for people across the United States.

In many of his works, Segal refers to art as well as to life. At the same time as we empathize with the characters in *The Gas Station*, we can give ourselves aesthetic distance by seeing the striding garageman as a contemporary version of Rodin's John the Baptist and his bushed helper as a reflection of the Barberini Faun.

Before Segal's trip to Paris, the back wall of the sculpture had been littered with the signs and messages typically found in service stations. As Segal later related, "Originally the whole thing was plastered with those brilliant fluorescent posters you find in these places. Then I stripped it down to achieve the effect of desolation I

34. *Alice Listening to Her Poetry and Music*, 1970
Plaster, wood, glass, and tape recorder, 96 x 96 x 33 in.
Staatsgalerie Moderner Kunst, Munich

35. *The Gas Station*, detail. See plate 36

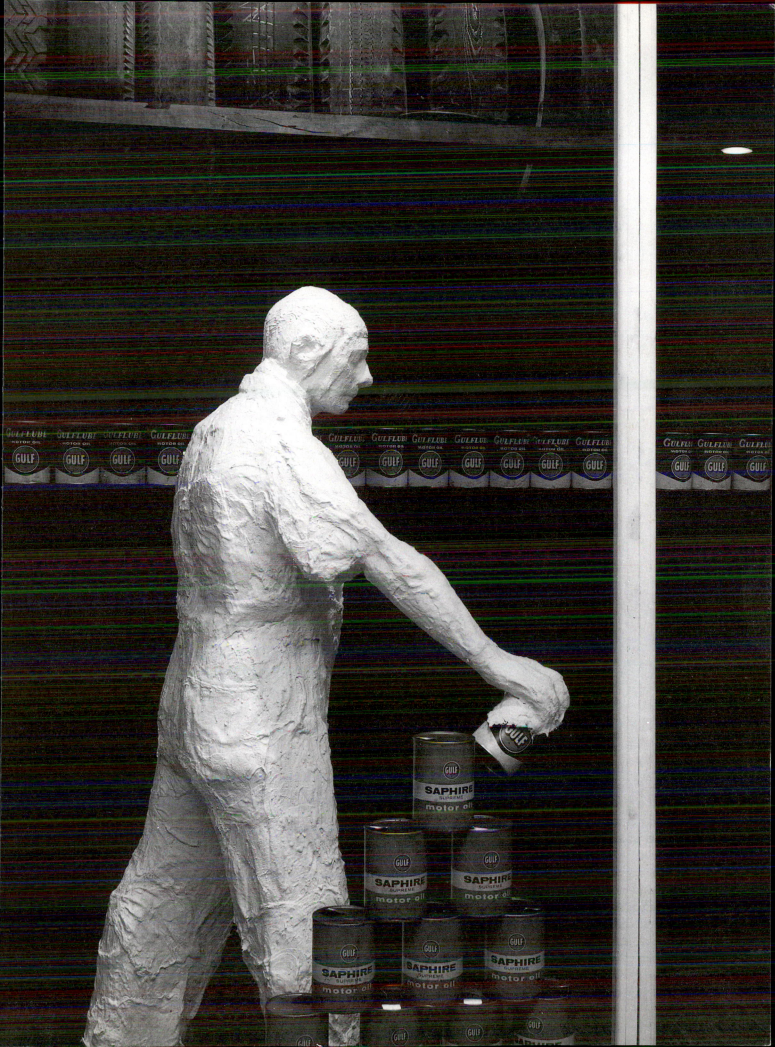

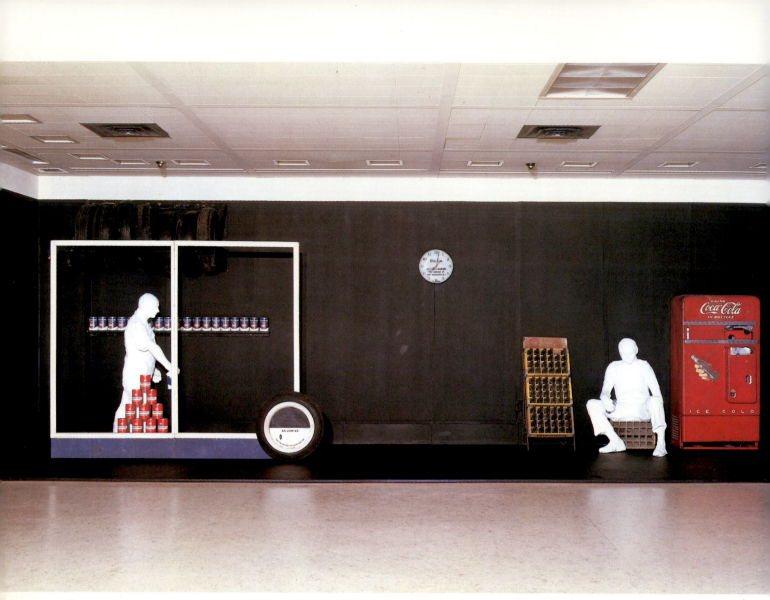

wanted."[31] The artist's Minimalist sensibility had overtaken his love of collage.

As the viewer walks around *The Gas Station*, each vantage point seems to present a new sculpture and a new meaning. When one contemplates the scene from the front, it reads benignly. But if one steps inside, other qualities become apparent. About the walking man, for example, Segal pointed out to Henry Geldzahler, "As you move around the glass, you encounter him from the rear and see a black rack of seven black tires suspended several inches above his head. This sudden catching of fright doesn't happen until you move into the right position and then you know him differently."[32]

In the small-enterprise sculptures, the number of figures and their varied poses affect a viewer's perception. We respond differently to the character we view from the back in *Cinema* than to the woman about to slaughter a chicken in *The Butcher Shop*. In Segal's art, the way someone stands or sits contributes meaning to a sculpture the way a verb completes a sentence.

In *The Diner*, the interaction between the two casts matters. A

36. *The Gas Station*, 1964
Plaster, metal, stone, glass, and rubber, 96 x 264 x 60 in.
National Gallery of Canada, Ottawa

37. *The Diner*, 1964–66
Plaster, wood, chrome, Formica, Masonite, and fluorescent light, 102 x 108 x 87 in.
Walker Art Center, Minneapolis
Gift of the T. B. Walker Foundation

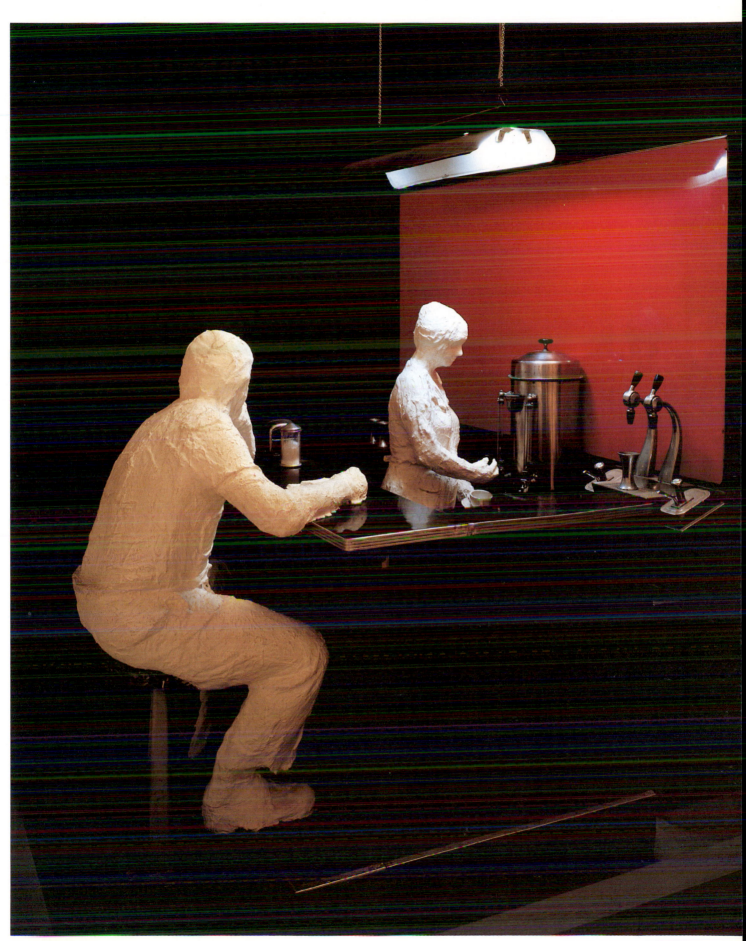

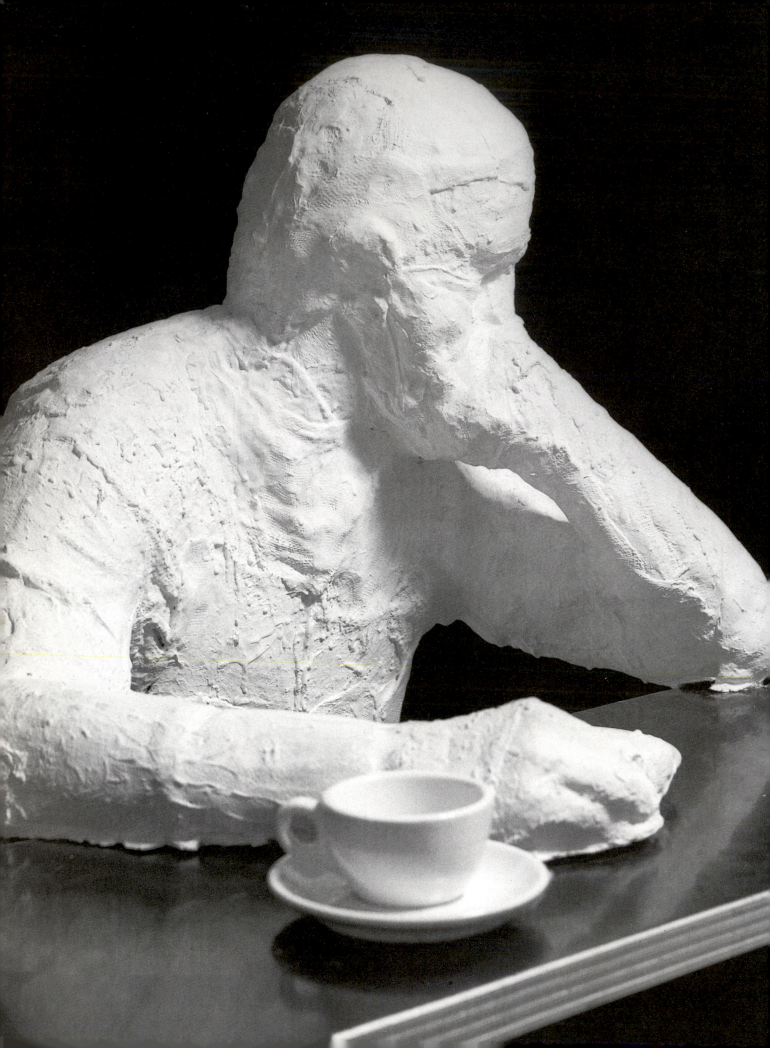

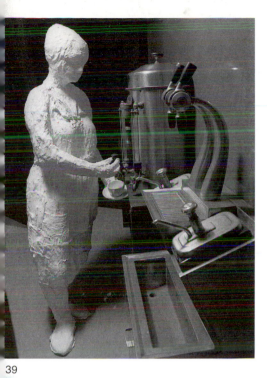

waitress fills a cup of coffee from a metal urn while a lone customer, his left hand on his cheek, sits on a leatherette stool at the counter. When first executed, the two figures were placed far apart. When the piece was returned to the artist's studio after his one-man show at the Sidney Janis Gallery in October 1965, Segal tightened the composition by moving the waitress and the urn close to her companion. In the first state, the man seemed to be staring at the attendant; later, his glance became less threatening by becoming more inner directed. At one time, the customer sat with a cup already at his place; in the current position, he waits to be served. Segal has said about *The Diner*, "I don't care about any specific soap opera that might be taking place . . . you can imagine 48 different plots."[33]

In *The Diner*'s sparse design, white, black, and red predominate. These dramatic shades are interrupted by the stainless steel equipment—urn, soda fountain, napkin dispenser, and the like—that reflects light from a harsh fluorescent fixture. "People zoom in on figures," the artist says. "They don't examine the shape and the weight and the presence of the so-called props, but I am not moved unless the figure, which is the shape of a certain gesture, combines with the feature of the so-called prop."

Segal seems to have captured a particular aspect of American highway life, like that chronicled by Willie Nelson's song, *On the Road Again*. His diner might be bleak, the people lonely, but the visual aspects of the scene are exhilarating because they are so masterfully handled. In terms of contemporary art, *The Diner* is located somewhere between roadhouse scenes by Edward Hopper and Edward Kienholz's *Barney's Beanery*. Such Hoppers lean toward illustration, while the Kienholz has a more surreal or funky flavor. Segal put it best when he said, "There's as much happening with abstract formality as there is with the literary or psychological . . . I'm trying to weave them together until they can't be separated."

The Dry-Cleaning Store also focuses attention on space, color, light, and surface. A plump attendant, bent over her counter, writes out a receipt. To her side, a large display case holds a plaster wedding gown. Hanging from the ceiling is a big neon "1-Hour Cleaning" sign made specially for the sculpture. The cast figure defines one space; the display case, another. Thus, two principal viewing positions are established. Unlike *The Gas Station*, there is a certain effect of transparency. Everything seems to open up. For example, the counter does not have closed-off sides. One looks through the neon sign. Air fills the display case.

Color and texture abound in the sculpture: the gray-painted figure, the wood counter, the display case with crinkly metallic paper, the red neon light, the white gown against a blue backdrop. In this situation the plastered dress seems real. Besides its formal complexities, *The Dry-Cleaning Store* also conveys commentary. This is as much a tale of marriage as *The Arnolfini Wedding* by Jan van Eyck. Wedding gowns are keepsakes, and here one hangs like a trophy. Segal once noted that in this metaphoric scene he was dealing with the loss of dreams and expectations. The woman at work here had probably once worn such a gown. As she floated down the aisle to the strains of Mendelssohn, her life was ahead of

39

38, 39. *The Diner*, details. See plate 37

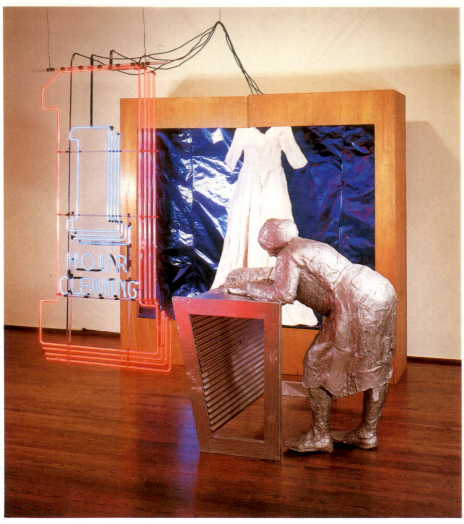

40

her. With the passing of time, her hopes might not have been fulfilled. Segal's sculptures are about truths, not fantasies.

Segal is among the many artists who have made art about art during the past two decades. The sculptures he executed on this theme during the 1960s touch upon the artist's creative life the way the scenes of small enterprise address his daily life in and around New Brunswick. Those completed during the 1970s and '80s are loving re-creations of art work he has admired.

John Chamberlain, burly and large-spirited, had been storing one of his automobile-part sculptures on Segal's land. As a joke, he volunteered to be cast with his work. Soon afterward, he posed wearing a welder's mask, with his arms outstretched in a bear hug. In *John Chamberlain Working* (1965–67), two styles of sculpture —metal construction and cast plaster—compete with one another. When it was first assembled, the multicolored, massive sculpture with deep pockets of space made the plaster figure look bland and fragile. So, Segal trimmed pieces of metal off the Chamberlain sculpture and covered figure and art with the same coat of paint, a strategy that Anthony Caro had used during the 1960s to balance disparate parts and metals. Like Caro, Segal found that he had equalized all the elements into a totality.[34]

41

Walking Man (1966) does not at first seem to belong to the 42
artists-at-work series. Painter Larry Poons, who posed for the piece
as if he were standing by a loft building gate, is not identified in
the title because this is not a conventional portrait. "Pretend you're
cold, hunch your shoulders," Segal said to his Green Gallery col-
league. Segal has made many sculptures with people walking, and
several have figures in front of doorways. In this instance, he wryly
used a metal grate whose patterning has a passing similarity to
Poons's dot paintings, and the red field against which the white
plaster figure and the black metal are seen also recalls his canvases.
By thus suggesting connections with his friend's art, Segal reminds
us that in our everyday surroundings we too may often pass commonplace images that resemble art.

Segal preferred not to take commissions during the 1960s. The
exceptions were portraits of art collectors Vera List, Robert Scull
(*Man with a Car Door*), and Scull with his wife, Ethel. Thus, Segal 44
was surprised when he was asked to cast his dealer: "Here is
Sidney Janis, whom I had always relied upon to shield me from
commissions, himself wanting to be portrayed."[35] He was delighted when Janis offered to provide his favorite display easel,
and on it, a treasured Mondrian. The plaster figure looks at the 43

41

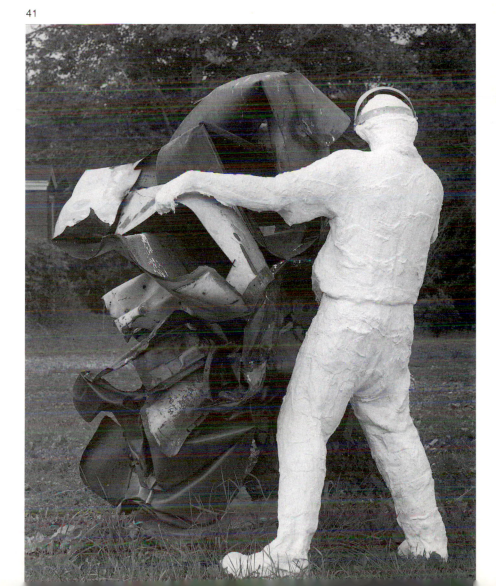

40. *The Dry-Cleaning Store*, 1964
Plaster, wood, metal foil, and neon light,
96 x 108 x 86 in.
Moderna Museet, Stockholm

41. *John Chamberlain Working*, 1965–67
Plaster and steel (unpainted state), 69 x
53 x 54 in.
Promised gift of Conrad Janis and Carroll Janis
to The Museum of Modern Art, New York

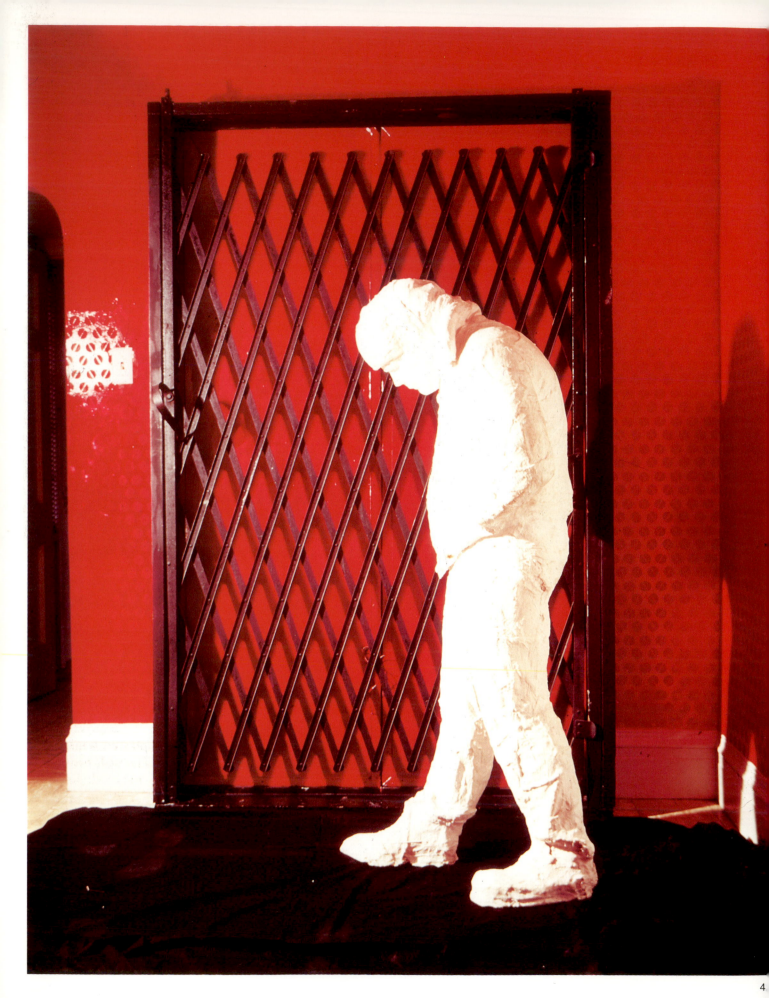

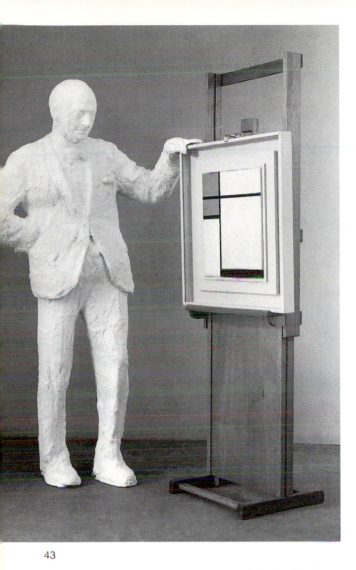

43

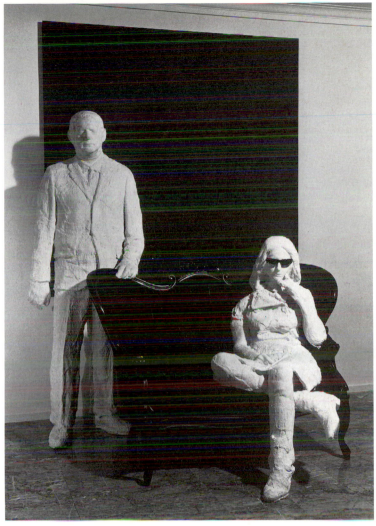

44

abstract masterpiece and we, in turn, look at the dealer and at the painting. The sculpture is a portrait as well as a record of one man's taste and discrimination. It also affirms Segal's high regard for Janis and for an early modern painter they both revere.

For convenience, Segal had posed anonymously for several of his own sculptures. In 1968, however, he executed two self-portraits, both representing different aspects of the processes that ordinarily lead to completed environments. In *The Artist in His Studio*, Segal is sketching on a table spattered with plaster, while male and female nudes pose on a plaster mattress. The wall near them is covered with black and white pastels, one of which includes a red chair back; all depict close-ups of the body. In the other self-portrait, the artist holds a girl's head not yet attached to the large-breasted figure perched on a chair. She calls to mind the life-size 1958 figure seated on an elegant chair. Seeing this work where past and present mingle, we realize how sophisticated Segal's art has become, and yet how indebted it is to the first ideas he had while making sculpture as a painter.

In 1970 Segal had the opportunity to view the great Matisse retrospective at the Grand Palais in Paris while the museum was closed to the public. One treat of this exposition was the opportunity to see the first version of *Dance*, owned by the Museum of

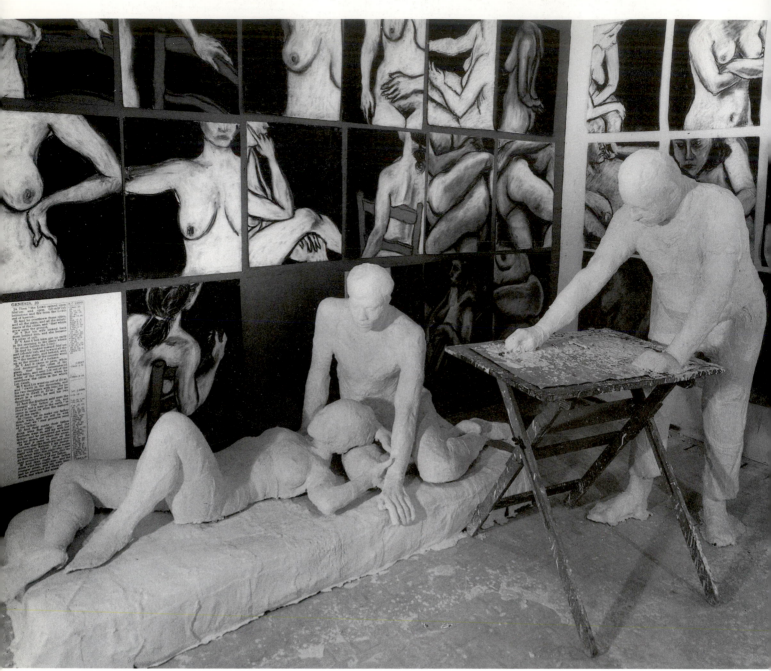

45

Modern Art in New York, alongside *Dance II*, its Russian mate
from the Hermitage Museum in Leningrad. A year after his return
47, 48 from Paris, Segal began his own *Dancers*, which he completed in
1973.

Instead of five dancers caroming around a green field and
outlined against a blue sky, Segal cast four women in a ring.
Rather than performing an animated Dionysian rite, they observe
a more measured pace. Where two figures in Matisse's painting
appear to have momentarily lost hold of one another's hands because of their whirling speed, the broader opening in Segal's sculpture invites a viewer to join the circle as the fifth and missing
dancer.

45. *The Artist in His Studio*, 1968
Plaster, wood, paper, and pastel, 96 x 120 x
108 in.
Galerie Onnasch, Cologne

46. *Self-Portrait with Head and Body*, 1968
Plaster and wood, 66 x 32 x 42 in.
Private collection

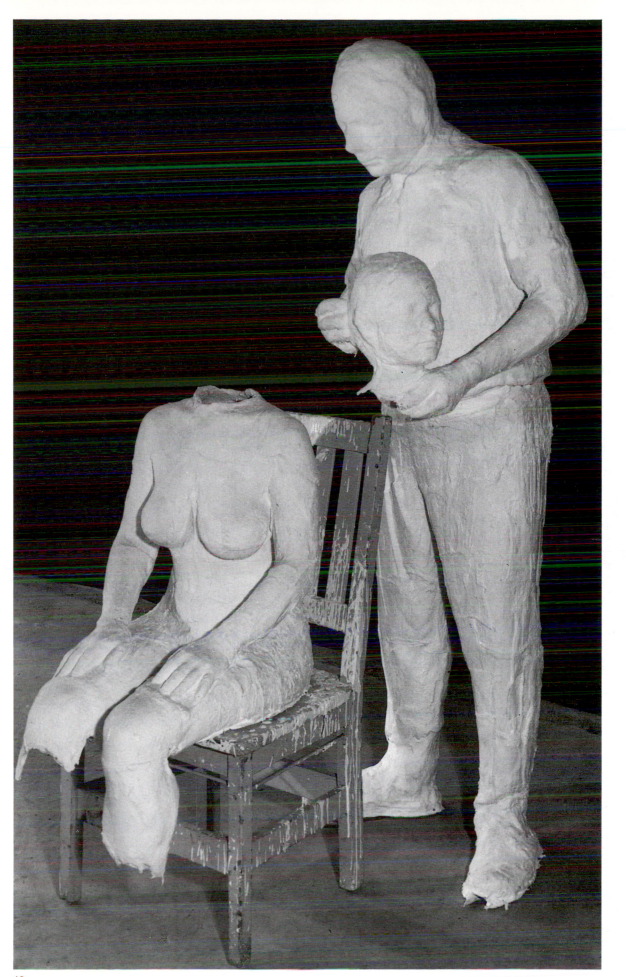

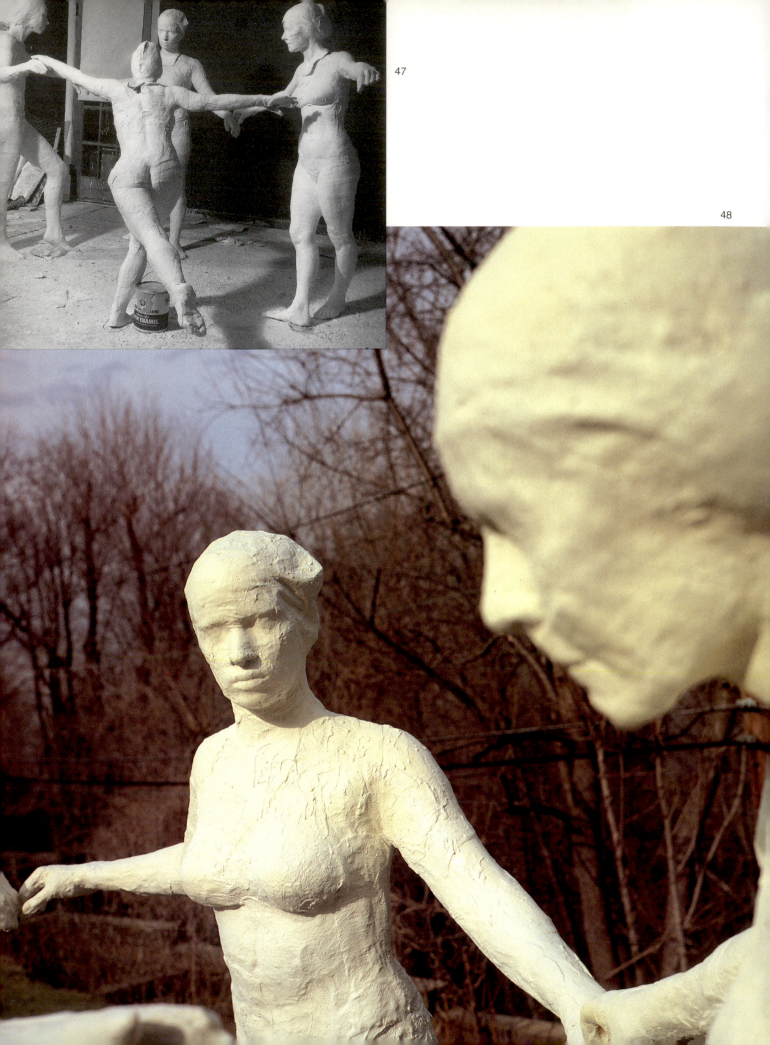

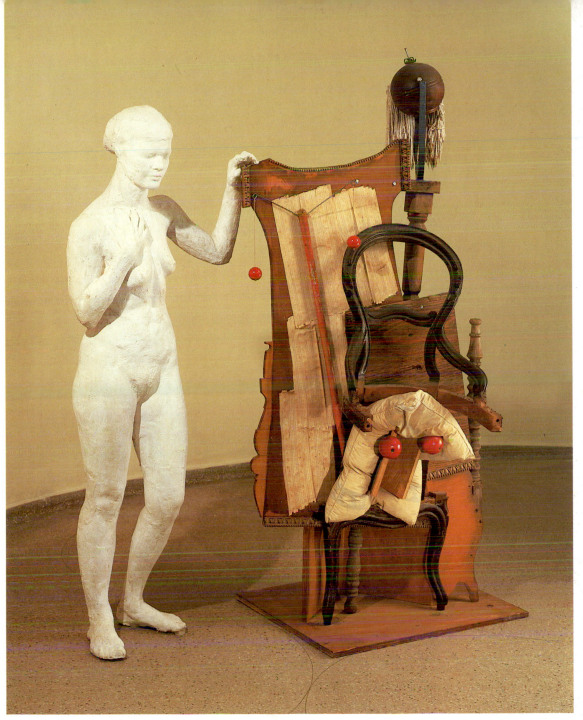

49

47.   *The Dancers*, 1971–73
Plaster and wood, 72 x 144 x 96 in.
Courtesy Sidney Janis Gallery

48.   *The Dancers*, 1971–82
Bronze, 72 x 144 x 96 in.
Private collection, Kings Point, New York

49.   *Picasso's Chair*, 1973
Plaster and mixed media, 78 x 60 in.
The Solomon R. Guggenheim Museum,
New York
Gift of Dr. Milton D. Ratner, 1976

No extraneous objects appear with the cast figures. Had Segal similarly isolated the garageman who resembles Rodin's *St. John the Baptist* from *The Gas Station*, his sculpture might have looked more like a statue. That is not the case here. Had we never seen Matisse's *Dance*, we would still find this the most convincing non-environment ever conceived by Segal. Nevertheless, now that *The Dancers* has been cast in white-patined bronze, its flirtation with statuary seems to account in some small way for its success in a more permanent material. When installed out-of-doors, *The Dancers* is silhouetted against land and sky like the Matisse. Segal's winsome performers then represent a "flat" picture transformed into a real-life situation. The result is a convincing sleight-of-hand.

Segal was also something of a magician when, in 1973, he re-
created in three dimensions Print No. 74 from the Vollard Suite,
executed by Picasso in 1933. Segal said about this piece: "So I
made *Picasso's Chair*, questioning the nature of things, hunting
for connections."[36] To the amazement of both Segal and his ad-
mirers, he did much more than find how "Picasso, that thundering
genius, had made a quick drawing" that could lead to a "sculpture
[that] stood up on its own legs."[37] It was not difficult for Segal
to cast a pretty girl with the serenity of the neoclassical model in
Picasso's print. Surprisingly, though, the Surrealistic chair/male
with its assertive presence and colorful parts appears more real
than the lithe plaster figure.

In 1981 and 1982 Segal created five still lifes based on paintings illustrated in the Time-Life Books edition of *The World of
Cézanne 1839–1906*. These colorful sculptures and reliefs were
the first he made without figures, and they reveal how inexhaustibly
inventive he can be. Segal used Cézanne's visual feasts as an excuse
to render cluttered surfaces and multihued images at a time when
his other works had fewer components than usual. While serving
as homages, these pieces also affirm their decidedly modern American origins: on the neck of one wine bottle, a Fetzer vineyard label
was left visible. Like other sculptures made by Segal during the
1980s, this group calls to mind his paintings of the 1950s and his

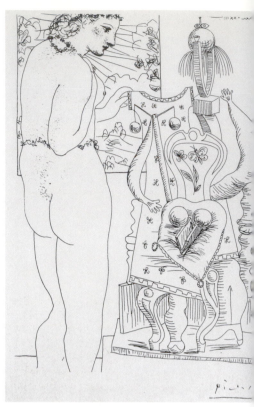

50

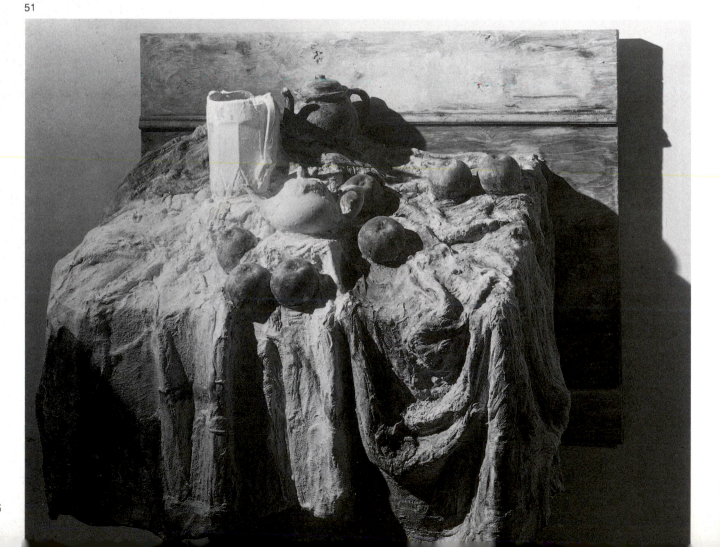

51

56

50. Pablo Picasso
No. 74 from the Vollard Suite, 1933
Etching on paper, 10½ x 7½ in.
The Solomon R. Guggenheim Museum,
New York
Gift of Dr. Milton D. Ratner, 1976

51. *Cézanne Still Life #2*, 1981
Painted plaster, wood, and metal, 32 x 40 x
14 in.
Courtesy Sidney Janis Gallery, New York

52. George Segal with *Cézanne Still Lifes*,
1982
Photograph by Allan Finkelman

53. *Cézanne Still Life #3*, 1981
Painted plaster, wood, and metal, 24 x 40 x
27½ in.
Courtesy Sidney Janis Gallery, New York

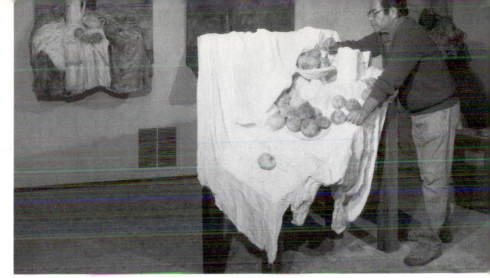

52

53

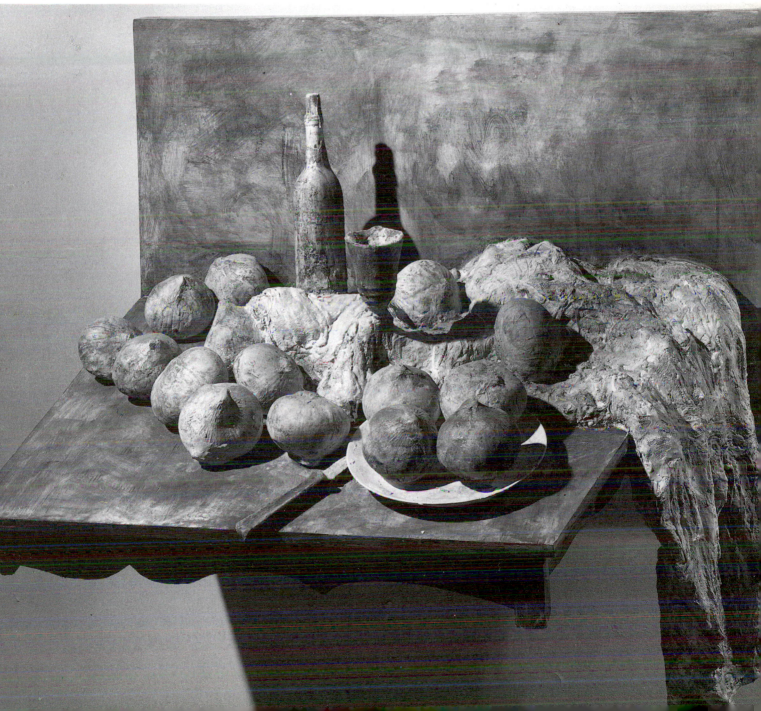

connections with the masters who first inspired him to become an artist.

For the most part, Segal's sculptures are welcoming rather than threatening. The figures that appear in them are gentle, the scenes comfortably familiar. Thus it was startling that during the mid-1960s Segal made three sculptures dealing with aspects of terror. *The Costume Party*, begun in 1965, unmasks psychological fears. *The Legend of Lot* of 1966 treats an apocalyptic, religious nightmare. *The Execution*, realized the following year, responds to the horrors of the Vietnam War. These hallucinatory tableaux all contain several cast figures; two of them depend on the relationships among characters rather than the inclusion of objects to create complicated situations. In each, plaster characters rest on the ground.

The Costume Party is a chilling arrangement of three men and three women who might have been encountered, according to Segal, at "an artist's party in a loft in the midst of the joyous rock of the '60s."[38] The sculptor once noted that he was incorporating into this piece "tension, confrontation, urgency with one's own feelings, no respect for masters, competition, anger, and no talk."[39] *The Costume Party* is a sculptural equivalent of the get-the-guest atmosphere that pervades Edward Albee's *Who's Afraid of Virginia Woolf?*

The Costume Party has been exhibited and photographed in at least five different states. Although the identity of the characters has remained the same, the placement of the figures, their coloration, and the props they wear have been continually varied. Discussing this unlikely gathering, Segal told an interviewer in 1965 that the theme "left me free to range from contemporary experience to Greco-Roman metamorphosis of man to beast. It's illustrative of the many faces between man and woman in the nature of reality as I see it."[40] The artist also said that he was much influenced when he made this sculpture by George Bernard Shaw's *Man and Superman* and by the philosophy of Nietzsche.[41]

When first exhibited, the cast of *The Costume Party* defined the four corners of a space. The self-enclosed work was about the kind of confrontation that transpires in a group therapy session. Later, when photographed outdoors, the figures were arrayed as if on a shallow stage addressing an audience. Today, the characters are bunched close together. When the viewer stands at the side of the masked man, the one figure who faces all the others, he or she is transformed from passive observer to active participant. At that moment, the sculpture functions the way the artist intended. Subject, formal composition, and meaning all lock into place.

The Legend of Lot occupies a curious position in Segal's oeuvre. None of the forty-three sculptures that preceded it prepares us for encountering a specific episode from the Old Testament. The artist, however, transformed into three dimensions the theme he had treated in his series of paintings exhibited at the Hansa Gallery in 1958.

Lot, sprawled drunkenly across a mattress laid on the ground, is being mounted by one of his daughters. Another daughter, awaiting her turn, watches her father and sister copulate. The mother,

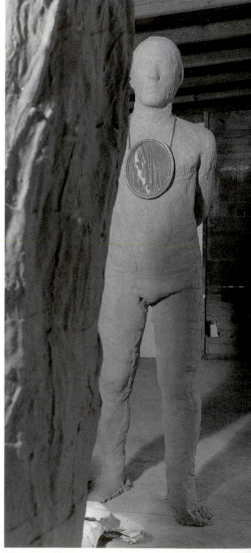

54

58

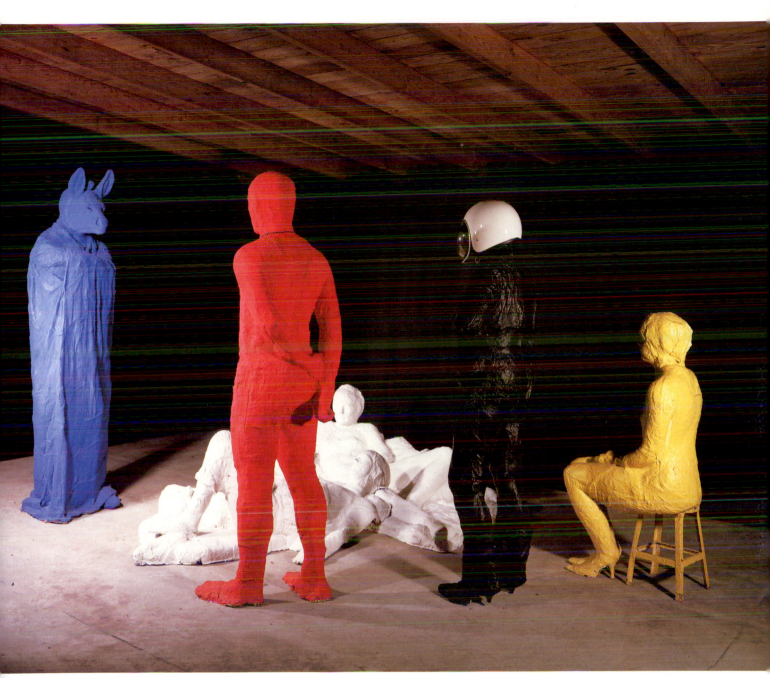

55

55. *The Costume Party*, 1965–73
Painted plaster, wood, glass, photograph, and
plastic, 72 x 144 x 108 in.
Collection of the artist

off to the side, her back to the scene, is at that moment turning
into a pillar of salt.

The Legend of Lot cannot be faulted formally. The figures are
convincing. There are a variety of poses and they suit the action.
The space has been fashioned with great care. A viewer looks
down, across, and away. It has never been made clearer that Segal
does not need objects to produce a gripping environment. But the
subject matter is so horrific, and so moralistic, that the role of the
participant has been altered drastically. Instead of being an observer, one comes away from *The Legend of Lot* feeling like a
voyeur. Consequently, the content dominates all other elements.
The careful, subtle integration of religious meaning into other

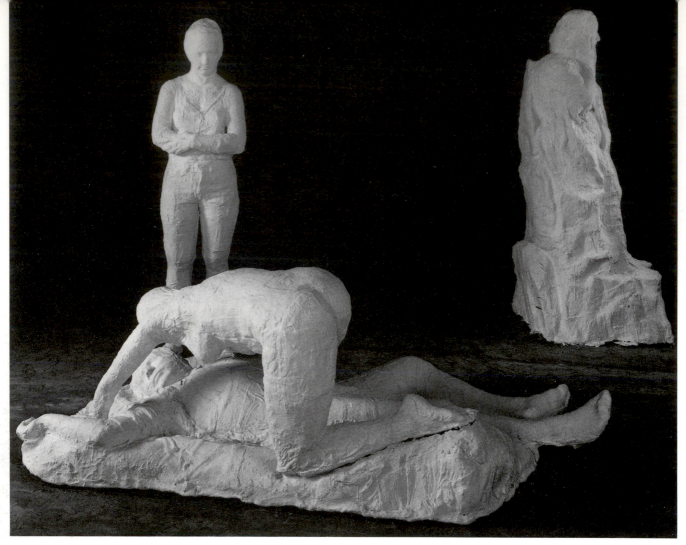

56

environments is out of kilter here. In *The Legend of Lot*, Segal
became an illustrator rather than a visual poet of metaphor.

Soon after the completion of *The Legend of Lot*, the New School
for Social Research asked Segal to participate in an exhibition
eventually called *Protest and Hope*. For this, he conceived *The
Execution*, the most resolved and effective of the three horror-
stricken works made between 1965 and 1967. On the left, a male
hangs upside down from his ankles, his arms stretched out as if
pinned to a cross, against a plywood wall stuccoed to resemble
concrete and riddled with bullet holes. The ground is littered with
three corpses, two women and a man. This emblematic sculpture
is as concise as a propaganda poster.

The Execution was designed with specific images in mind. Segal
was familiar with photographs of Mussolini's public humiliation.
He also remembered a predella panel from the *Martyrdom of St.
Peter* by Masaccio, which had been exhibited in New York in
1948. The artist told an interviewer, "The most monumental painting I ever saw was Masaccio's *Martyrdom of St. Peter*, which is
about four inches square. . . . Monumentality shouldn't be con-
fused with a monument."⁴² Having voiced this admonition, he
nevertheless achieved such a synthesis in *The Execution*, a contemporary Last Judgment. The artist once suggested that in this piece

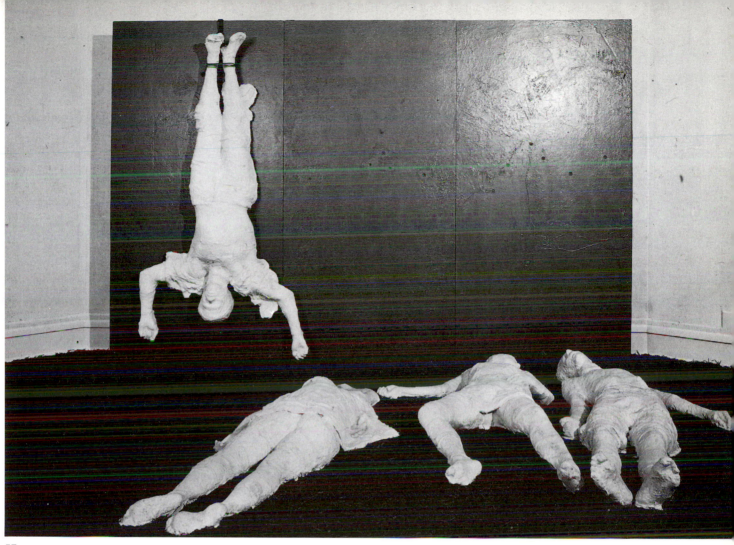

57

56. *The Legend of Lot*, 1966
Plaster, 72 x 96 x 108 in.
Kaiser Wilhelm Museum, Krefeld
Sammlung Lauffs

57. *The Execution*, 1967
Plaster, wood, metal, and rope, 96 x 132 x 96 in.
Vancouver Art Gallery

he let the viewer feel that "you too can be both aggressor and victim."[43] For Segal, there has never been any question that man is a political animal and that, occasionally, art can lend its values to a moral cause.

By balancing subject matter, abstract design, and philosophical or psychological content, Segal has endowed his sculpture with the force of Old Master paintings, in which realism, formal composition, and iconography were carefully integrated. There have been certain sculptures by Segal, though, in which subject matter has overpowered the other elements. In other works, content has seemed the most compelling. Thus, it is not surprising to discover a category of sculptures dominated by a formal device: illumination. After *Cinema* and *The Dry-Cleaning Store*, Segal's innovative use of various types of electric light evolved to the degree that it enhances meaning in a number of environments.

When Segal incorporated fluorescent tubes, neon signs, and naked bulbs into his art, he did not use them as avant-garde gimmickry merely for their own sake, even though he was obviously indebted to Happenings, which had made it possible for an artist to use manufactured light. In Segal's hands, light has defined space, created atmosphere, and offered an element of narration.

In *The Photobooth* (1966) and *The Moviehouse* (1966–67) Segal 58, 59

61

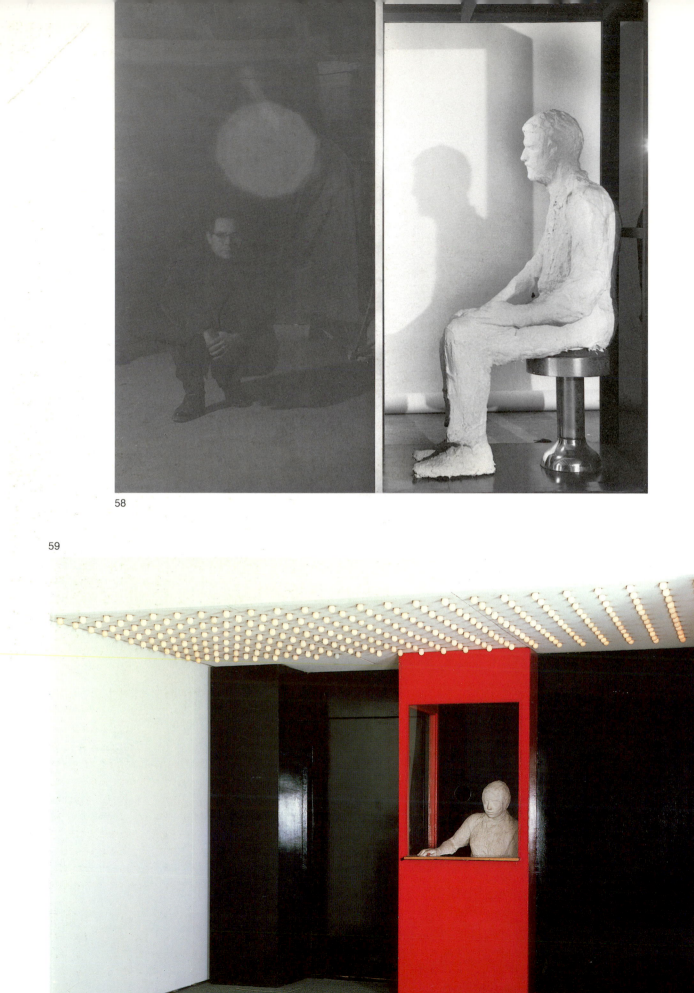

58

59

62

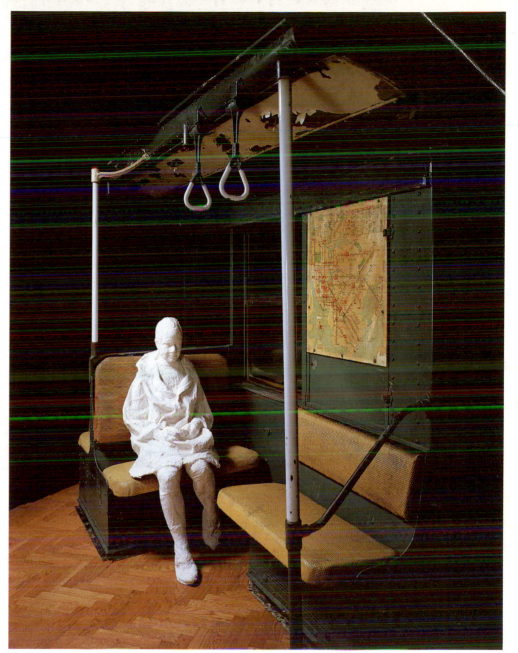

60

used electric lights to help structure his compositions. Allan Kaprow posed in the five-and-dime store machine of *The Photobooth*. A tall, bearded man, he sits solemnly regarding the harshly lit glass through which the camera operates. The sculpture's action takes place within the confines of the photo machine, and the viewer must peer into the booth to see what is going on. *The Photobooth* deals with depiction and reflection. It is a sculpture about cheap photography in an age of mechanical reproduction. When posing, a person studies himself or herself in a mirrored surface. At the same time, reflection of another sort transpires as light enlivens the shiny black metal walls that entomb the sitter.

In *The Moviehouse*, light was again deployed in tandem with a boxed figure. With her hand outstretched to collect money, a ticket-seller sits in a red booth behind a glass partition. White lights radiate off the cantilevered marquee, and the canopy of 288 six-watt incandescent bulbs heats anyone beneath its shower of illumination. Segal's scene presents the burst of light we encounter before being plunged into the darkness of the theater.

As the 1960s drew to a close, Segal's casting process and his skills in constructing environments became ever more sophisticated. Electric light came to function in ways not previously anticipated. In *The Subway* (1968), a young girl sits quietly on a worn bench in a mass-transit car that seems to be hurtling along its route. But, the train is as stationary as the subway map and the bare light bulb. When he was initially designing this environment (and wending his way through bureaucratic channels to obtain the retired car), Segal shot a super-8mm. film between stations in the Manhattan subway. He had expected to loop the material (as he had done in *The Truck* of 1966), so that looking through the windows one would see what one normally saw while riding the IND or the IRT. However, the artist found that his home movie did not have enough clarity. So, behind the car, he fashioned a system of light bulbs regulated by a revolving wheel that determines how the lights blink on and off. Thus, electric lights ingeniously create the sense of movement in *The Subway*.

In 1970 Segal wanted to depict a distant vista glimpsed as if from an airplane. On his drives at night to and from New York, he would not only see the Manhattan skyline lit up in the distance, he would also pass the fields of Newark Airport. To recreate such scenes in his sculptures meant that for the first time he would be suggesting deep space, an illusion easier to achieve on a painted surface through the laws of perspective. The solution proved to be simpler than expected. In *The Aerial View* hundreds of holes were drilled in a plywood board so that colored, light-conducting pegs could be mounted in a pattern derived from slides the artist had shot one evening during a round-trip helicopter ride between Newark and Kennedy airports. Lit from the rear, a panorama unfolds before the standing cast figure and the viewer, who feels as if he or she is this man's companion. While the depicted environment was specific to Segal, it is so general in nature that it would be familiar to drivers entering Phoenix from Camelback Mountain, for example, or Los Angeles from Mulholland Drive.

Once he had devised the means to create deep space, Segal also made, in 1970, *Times Square at Night* and *Girl Leaning against a Doorway*. Night scenes along city streets, these are brother/sister environments. In *Times Square*, two male hustlers amble beneath the marquee of a porno palace and a well-known coffee shop named, a bit ironically, Childs. The artist also included the letter Z, the title of the then-current Costa-Gravas political film, as well as the symbol of Zorro, the swashbuckling hero of movies and television. By using light as a crucial element in the definition of this environment, Segal not only captured the dead of night, he also accentuated the backlit words and letters that enhance the work's content.

By 1976 Segal's environments had become rather sparse, stripped of all but the most essential objects. In *Walk—Don't Walk*, a blinking light mounted on the cement curb of a street corner both structures the scene and gives it meaning. Besides adding a touch

61. *Times Square at Night*, 1970
Plaster, wood, plastic, and electrical parts,
108 x 96 x 60 in.
Joslyn Art Museum, Omaha, Nebraska

62. *The Aerial View*, 1970 (p. 66)
Plaster, wood, plastic, incandescent and
fluorescent light, 96 x 104 x 48 in.
Sara Hilden Art Museum, Tampere, Finland

63. *Walk—Don't Walk*, 1976 (p. 67)
Plaster, cement, metal, painted wood, and
lights, 104 x 72 x 72 in.
Whitney Museum of American Art, New York
Gift of the Louis and Bessie Adler Foundation,
Inc., the Gilman Foundation, Inc., the Howard
and Jean Lipman Foundation, Inc., and the
National Endowment for the Arts

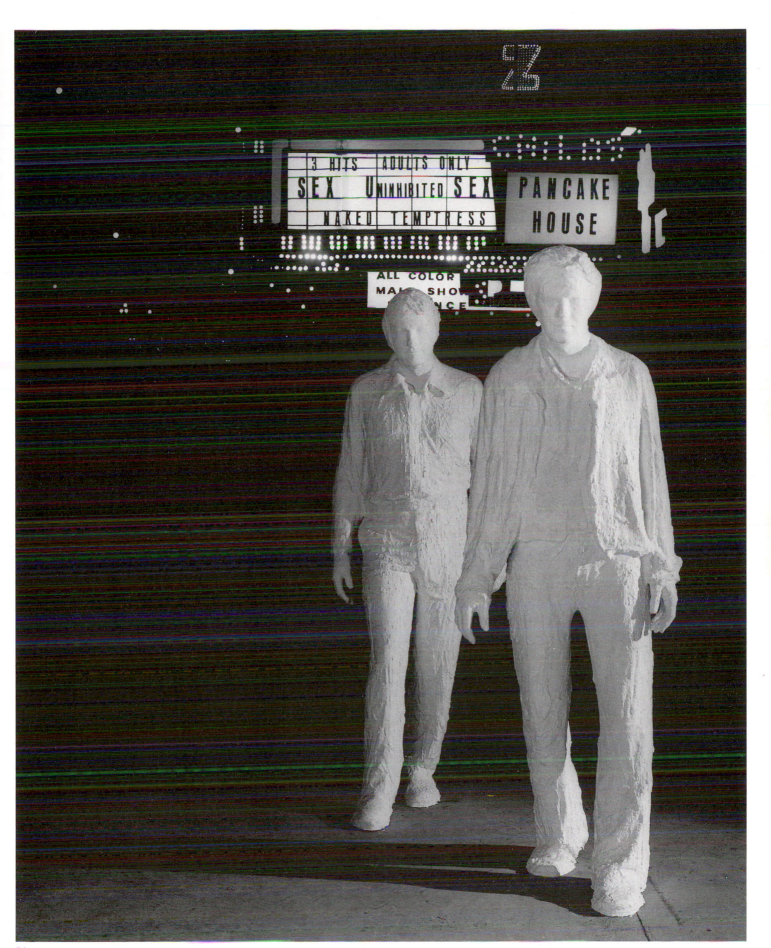

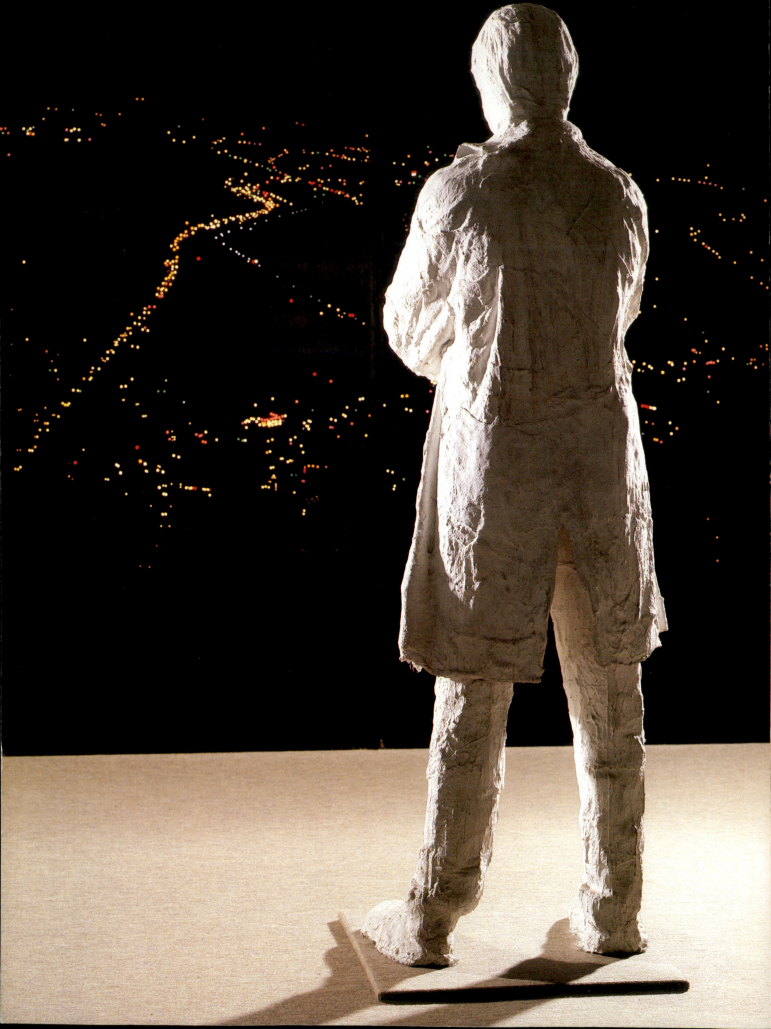

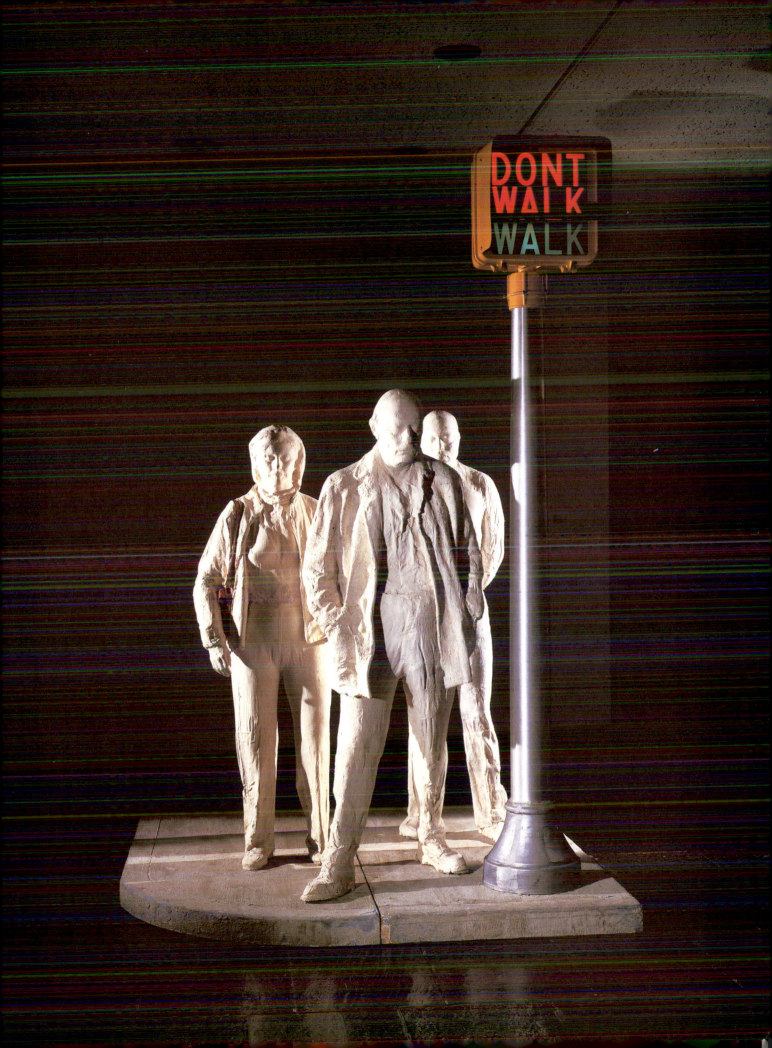

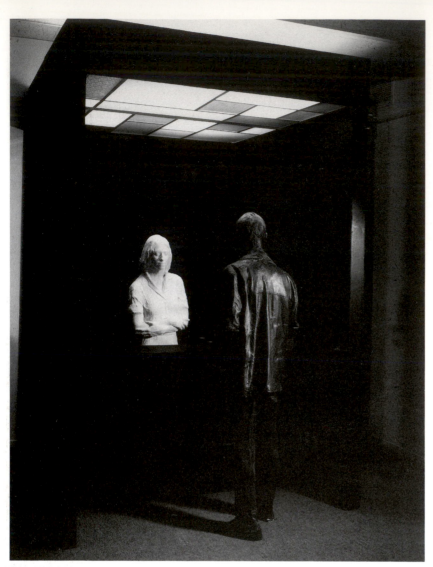

64

of color to the sculpture, the sign also explains why these three people have momentarily gathered together. In a work like *The Moviehouse*, Segal had arranged colored planes as if constructing a three-dimensional painting by Mondrian; here the classic balance between figures and object more subtly recalls the artist's love for the principles of early abstraction. The traffic sign in *Walk—Don't Walk*, like the hi-fi equipment in *Girl Listening to Music*, tellingly underscores how Segal redirected the ideas behind Happenings to create an enduring image rather than an ephemeral experience.

Manufactured light also played important roles in two sculptures dealing with dance: *Go-Go Dancer* of 1978 and *The Hustle: The Four-Hand Pass* of 1980. In both, mirrors reflect countless patterns of light and seem to set the cast figures in motion. Nineteen show lights rim the mirror of *Go-Go Dancer* and intensify the garishness of her lewd pose. In *The Hustle: The Four-Hand Pass*, a rotating mirrored light turns rhythmically to suggest the fast paces of the elderly, bow-tied male and his young, nubile partner. In these instances, one could hardly say that Segal has frozen time because the figures seem so active.

64. *The Hot Dog Stand*, 1978
Painted plaster and painted wood with plastic, metal, and electric lights, 108 x 72 x 81½ in.
San Francisco Museum of Modern Art
T. B. Walker Foundation and Clinton Walker Funds Purchase

65. *The Hustle: The Four-Hand Pass*, 1980
Plaster, wood, plastic, metal, video tape and sound, sound studio: 96 x 144 x 192 in.; figures: 68 x 38 x 38 in.
Courtesy Sidney Janis Gallery, New York

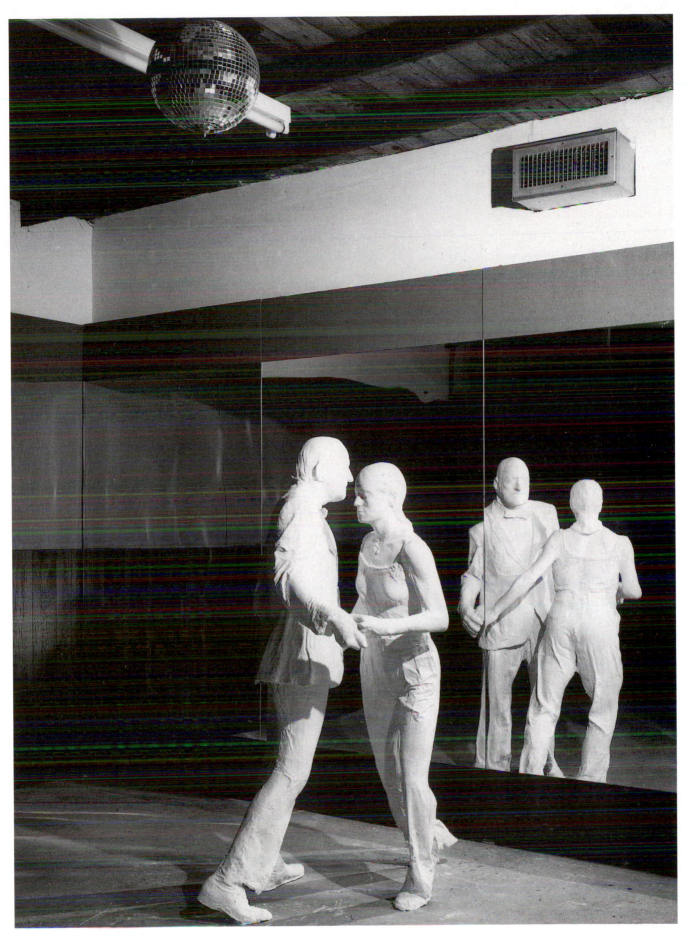

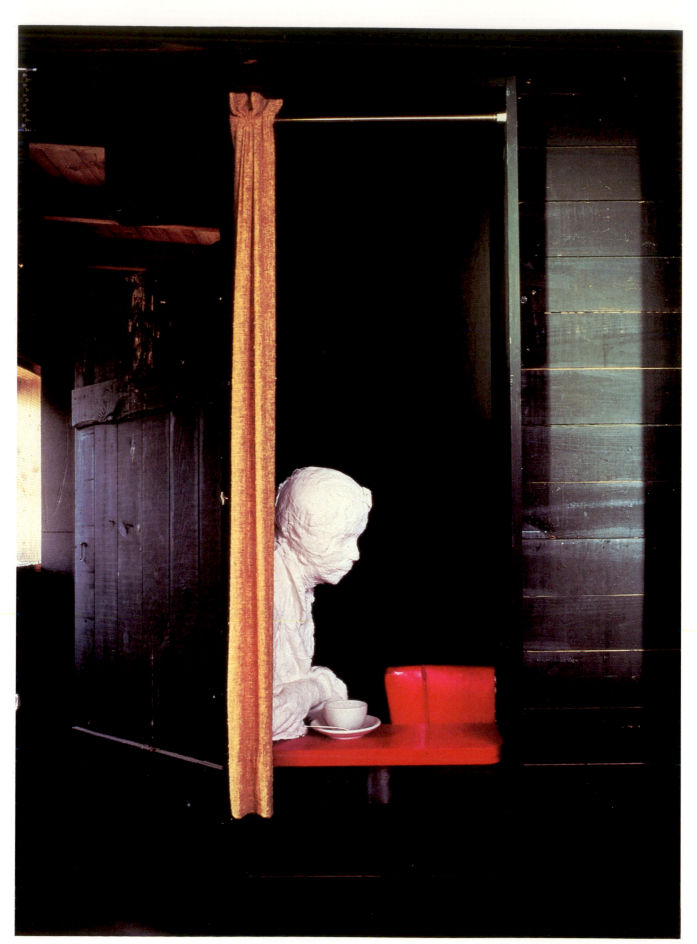

4 Fragments and Painted Plasters

For more than seven years, Segal's studio contained piles of unassembled molds. Most were eventually transformed into completed sculptures, others simply became rejects. Then, in 1969, he began to make these body parts into independent works: truncated torsos were placed in wall boxes and anatomical fragments became reliefs. Segal refers to these as "independent thoughts or sensations."[44]

Five boxes and twenty fragments were included in Segal's show at the Sidney Janis Gallery during May 1970. Sixty inches tall, 24 inches wide, and 12 inches deep, each box was large enough to include objects and small enough to call a viewer's attention to a figure's gesture and mood. Like the walk-in environments, these magnified scenes present contrasts between white plaster surfaces and the colors of all other components.

The fragments were of another sort. With irregularly edged profiles, these reliefs are composed with details of breasts and buttocks, shoulders and chins. Representation and abstraction have never been more tersely synthesized by Segal. About these, he commented: "The fragments must have begun from some kind of erotic or sensual impulse, to define bits of lips, fingers, breasts, folds of flesh, intricate lines."[45]

Segal also credits the creation of boxes and fragments to his "questioning about the nature of twentieth-century collage . . . I discovered that the thing I liked about collage is not the way it's scattered so musically over the surface, but the fact that each piece of collage seems to me a glimpse, a rapid glimpse out of the corner of my eye." He explained further, "When I walk down a street and I notice something, I notice it in a glimpse . . . I thought, what happens if I do a piece of the body and try to catch that piece of gesture that moves me?"[46]

Once a work like *Lovers II* (1970) is completed, it actually exists more as a close-up than a glimpse. It seems more than coincidental that Segal was concurrently designing environments that for the first time suggested deep vistas. Thus, two different spatial systems were suddenly operative in his art.

The fragments became increasingly sensuous and more erotic, a far cry from the initial group of boxes. Some are practically abbre-

66. *The Coffee Shop*, 1969
Plaster, wood, metal, plastic, and fabric,
60 x 24 x 12 in.
Private collection

69

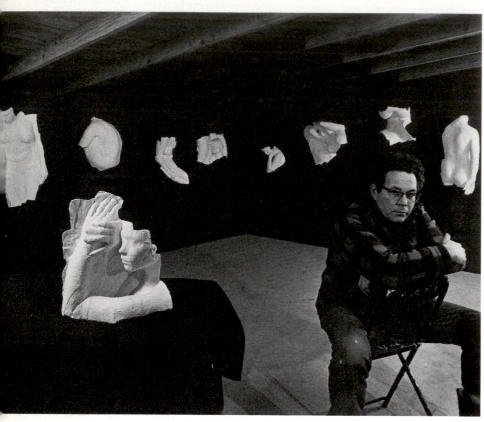

67

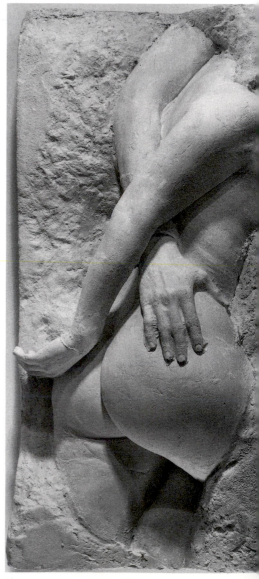

viated three-dimensional sculptures. *Lovers II*, for example, consists of two heads and chests that merge in a way that recalls Brancusı's *The Kiss* of 1911. In other, later fragments, anatomies with smooth skins, large breasts, and svelte derrières appear to be emerging from matter itself in the manner of marbles by Rodin. *Girl on Blanket, Hand on Leg* (1973) celebrates feminine form; at the same time, light flows across the sinuous curves while the rutted background captures pockets of shadows. Occasionally, the fragments project out from rough plaster surfaces. A work like *Crouching Woman* (1975) suggests comparison with Segal's pastels. However, with its swelling volumes, the headless relief seems to be about contained energy, something not as readily communicated by the flat paper works, which deal with color and outline. Where Segal's environments frequently reveal his Minimalist sensibility, his second group of reliefs has an orientation that is authentically classical, more on the order of Rodin and Maillol.

In the mid-1970s, Segal executed a number of wall works that combined the nature of the fragments with formats first developed in the boxes. In these, nudes appear behind barely opened colored doors. Earlier, in the *Girl in Robe* series of 1974, he had played with revealed and hidden properties. Now, pallor and hue contrast, as do the texture of wood and plaster. Many of these later pieces call to mind larger environments; but because they are more reduced, they revert to glimpses.

68

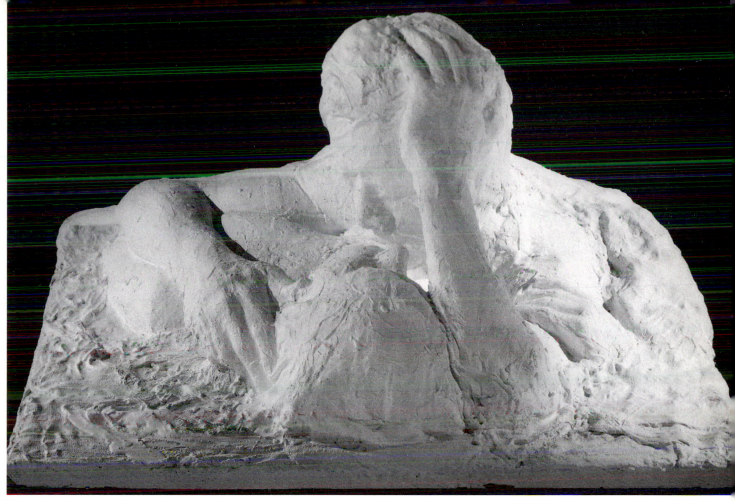

69

70

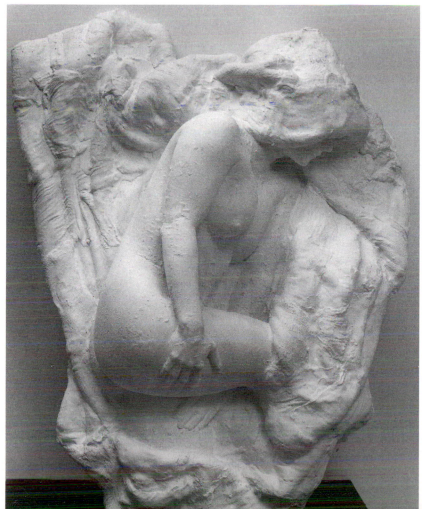

67. George Segal in his studio with fragments, 1970
Photograph by Hans Namuth

68. *Her Arm Crossing His*, 1975
Plaster, 40¼ x 18¼ x 12 in.
Witte Memorial Museum, San Antonio, Texas

69. *Lovers II*, 1970
Plaster, 36 x 24 x 24 in.
Private collection

70. *Girl on Blanket, Hand on Leg*, 1973
Plaster, 50 x 39 x 10 in.
Courtesy Sidney Janis Gallery, New York

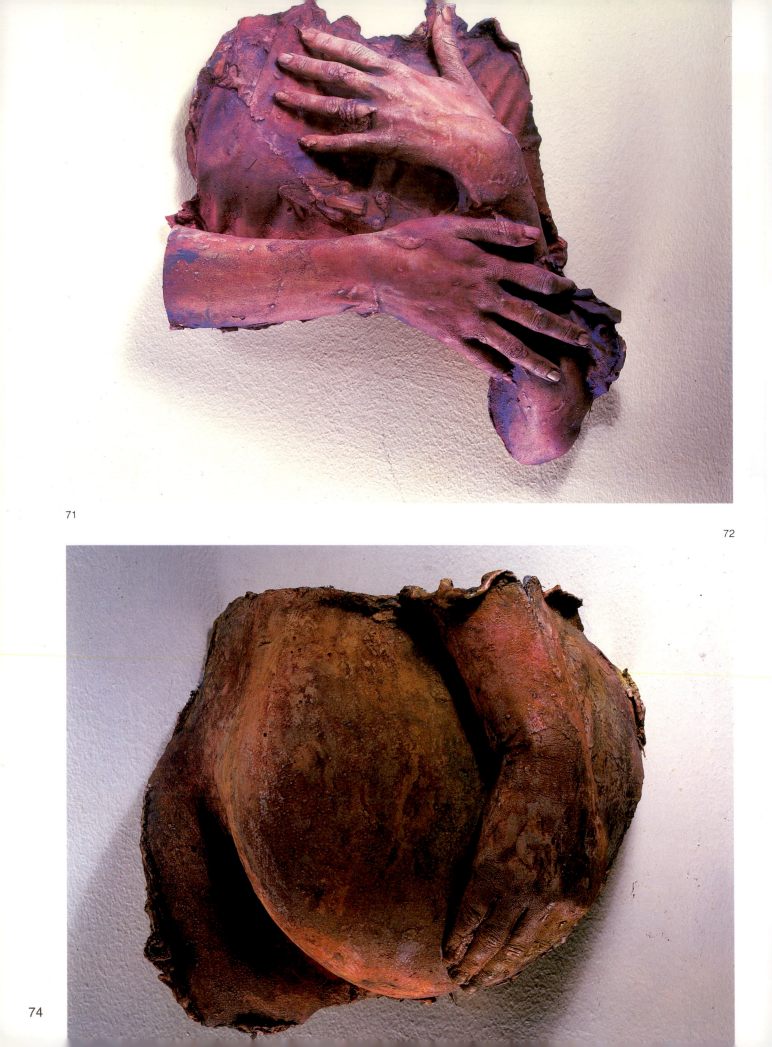

71

72

74

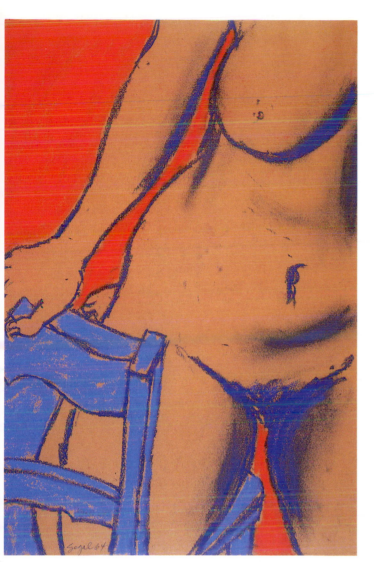

73

71. *Two Hands and Dress Buckle*, 1978
Painted plaster, 16 x 12 x 4½ in.
Courtesy Sidney Janis Gallery, New York

72. *Hand on Right Buttock*, 1978
Painted plaster, 12 x 11 x 6 in.
Courtesy Sidney Janis Gallery, New York

73. Untitled, 1964
Pastel on paper, 18 x 12 in.
Private collection

74. Untitled, 1964
Pastel on paper, 18 x 12 in.
Private collection

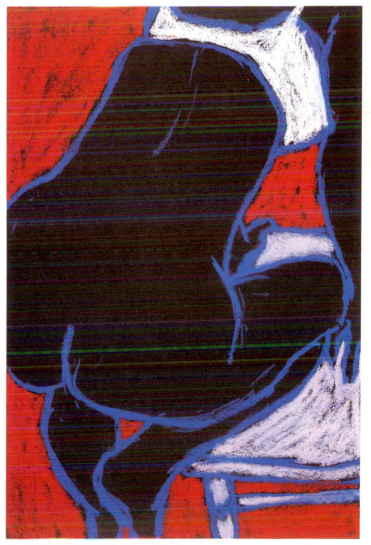

74

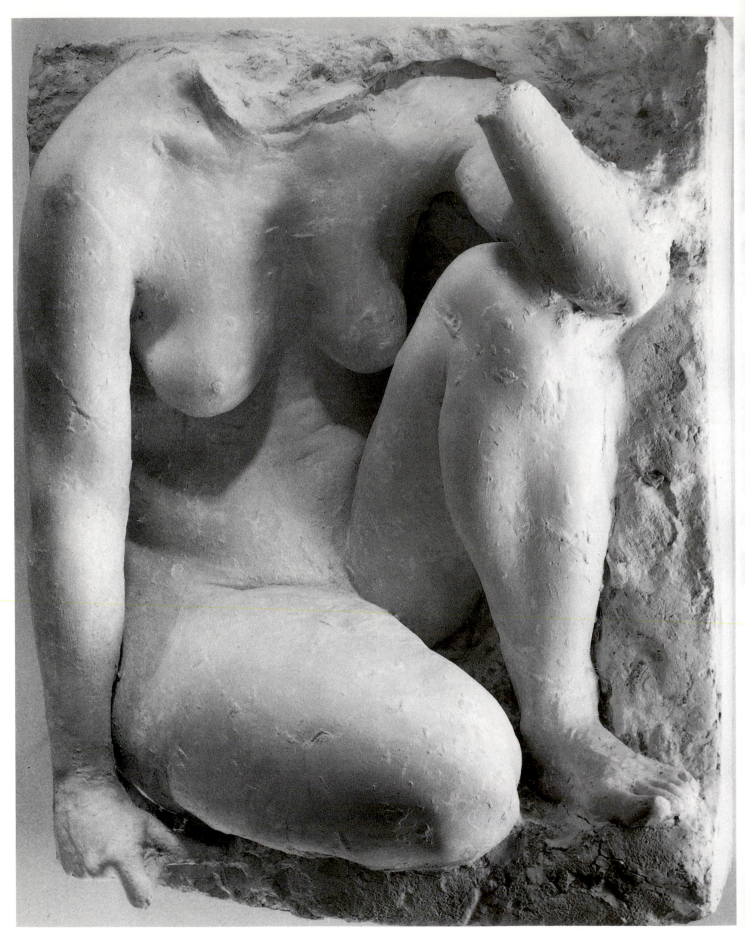

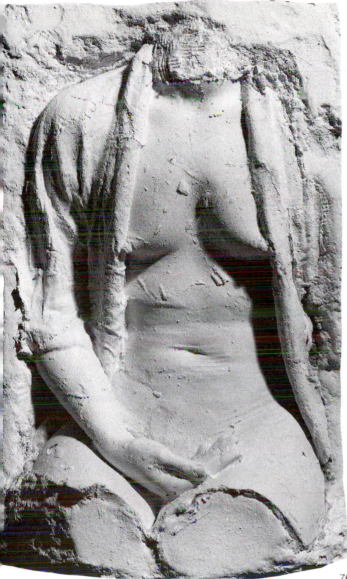

76

77

75. *Crouching Woman*, 1975
Plaster, 28 x 22½ x 16 in.
Courtesy Sidney Janis Gallery, New York

76. *Girl in Robe II*, 1974
Plaster, 29½ x 18 x 9½ in.
Courtesy Sidney Janis Gallery, New York

77. *Girl in Robe IV*, 1974
Plaster, 32 ¾ x 18¼ x 8½ in.
Courtesy Sidney Janis Gallery, New York

Restless invention characterizes the fragments and boxes because new formats and themes are constantly being introduced. *Three Bathers with Birch Tree* (1980), for example, is frontal in its treatment and thus feels more pictorial than other reliefs by Segal. As in Georges Seurat's *Les Poseurs*, three women are turned in different directions: front, back, and side. Rather than having to walk around an environment in order to regard all sides of a model, here one can, in effect, see several images simultaneously. A tree introduced into this work performs several functions. It suggests that this is an outdoor scene. It visually anchors the composition and most important, it transforms the models into goddesses in a forest, a new

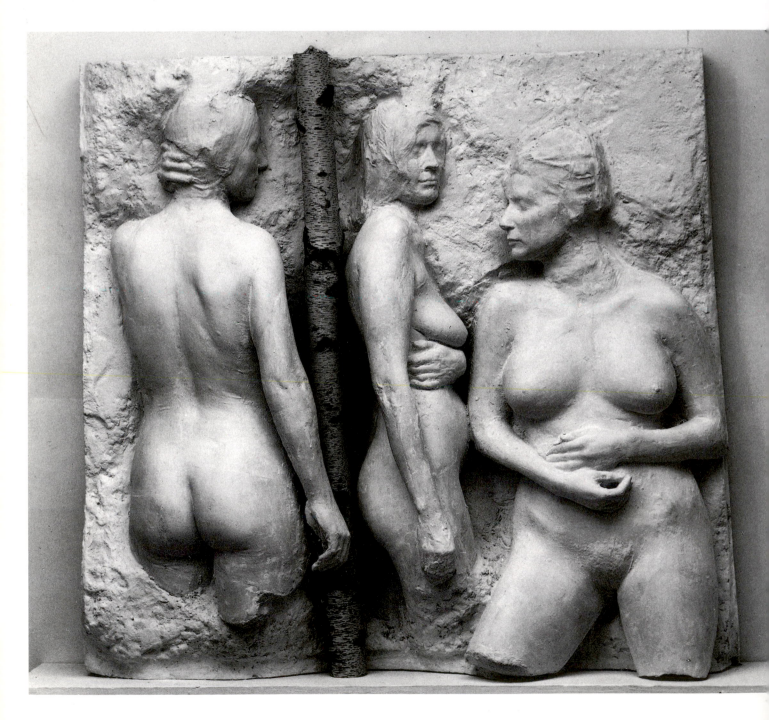

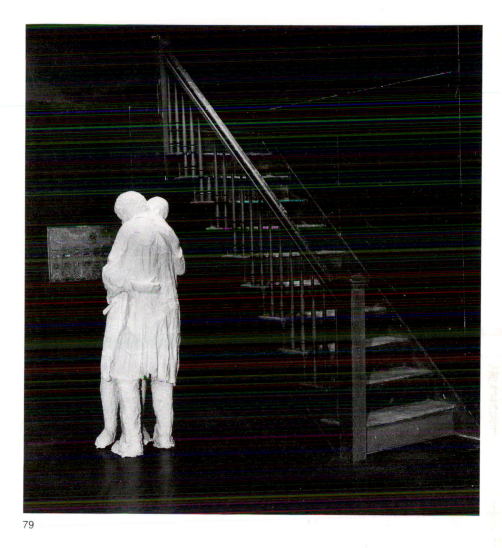

79

78. *Three Bathers with Birch Tree*, 1980
Plaster and wood, 72 x 64 x 14 in.
Private collection

79. *Couple at the Stairs*, 1964
Plaster, wood, and metal, 120 x 104 x 96 in.
Museum Bovmans-van Beuningen, Rotterdam

idea in the artist's oeuvre. Thus, meaning, not just form, is con-
cisely dealt with in this relief.

As Segal has developed his boxes and reliefs, a range of forms
and subjects that could hardly have been anticipated in 1969 has
become apparent. When dealing with truncated torsos and body
fragments, as in many of his other most recent works, George
Segal the sculptor is making use of his initial experiences as a
painter.

In 1976, when Segal began to work with bronze, his sculptures
for the first time had to be covered with another substance: a
patina. He subsequently began to color the plasters as well (although *The Costume Party* of 1966–73 had been painted, it remained an early, odd exception). At this juncture, his painter's
sensibility intersected with his skills as a sculptor. According to
Hilton Kramer, "Segal hit his stride once his chromatic inventive-
ness appeared."[47] Three particular themes proved especially suit-
able to being painted: lovers, figures in doorways, and people by
windows. These subjects had always been favorites of Segal's, and
they had appeared throughout his career as unpainted plasters in
such varied guises as *Couple at the Stairs* (1964), *Woman in a*   79, 80
Doorway I (1964), and *Lovers on a Bed II* (1970).   81

At first, Segal's polychrome sculptures owed a debt to pictorial ideas introduced by geometric hard-edge artists during the 1960s. His colors were flat and monochromatic. Soon, however, the sculptor's Abstract Expressionist tendencies began to resurface: many tones were mixed together and jarring contrasts abound.

83   Segal pointed out that *The Corridor* (1976), one of his first works with a painted figure, "was essentially a flat, black room, a yellow door, a blue figure of a girl and a red chair—a simple red chair. And, it was red, yellow, blue in a black space. The uninflected flat paint was something like a habitual hangover, habit, carryover of 1960s painting. . . ."[48] This naming of individual hues obscures how Segal's color works. When a plaster is painted, figure and objects become one and the same rather than coexisting as independent components.

Color also contributes to mood. "On one level, *The Corridor* is

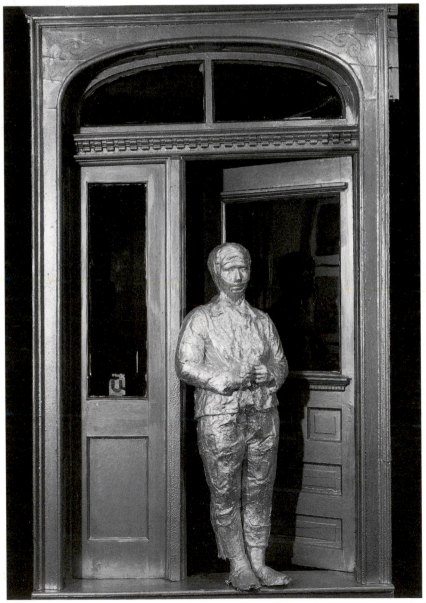

80. *Woman in a Doorway I*, 1964
Plaster, wood, glass, and aluminum paint,
113 x 63 x 18 in.
Whitney Museum of American Art, New York

81. *Lovers on a Bed II*, 1970
Plaster and metal, 48 x 72 x 60 in.
Philip Johnson

82. *Lovers on a Bed II*, detail

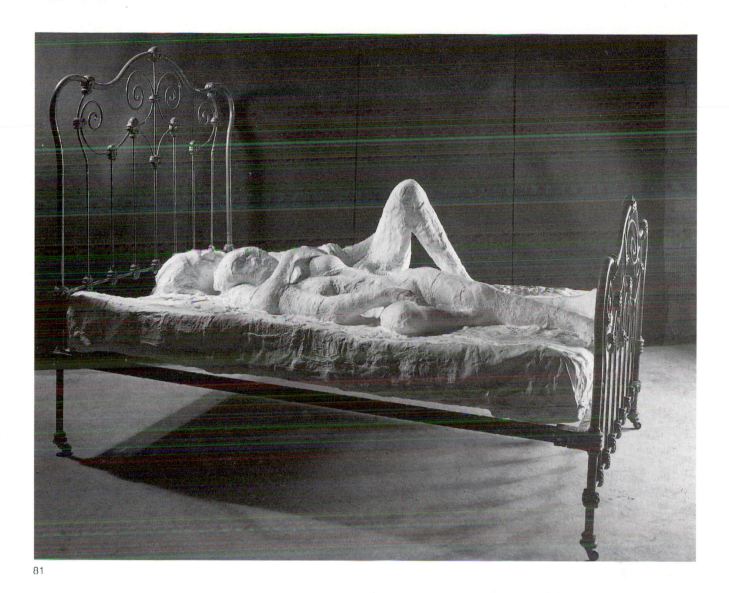

81

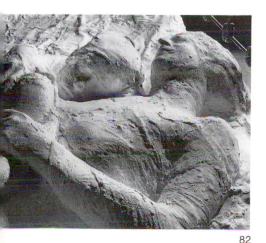

82

very sensual—the door is open and welcoming," the artist has related. "On the other hand, it's about the passage of time, and intimations of mortality."[49] Had the cast girl remained white, the psychological and the philosophic implications of this environment would not be as clear, nor as gripping.

Similar threads are woven together in *Blue Girl on Black Bed*, also 1976. The viewer can hardly remain a neutral observer when confronting a bed and slumbering male painted black and a woman seated on the edge of a mattress draped in blue. This haunting sculpture calls to mind such works by Picasso as *La Vie* (1903) and *Meditation* (1904). Segal emerges here as an expressionist, not a naturalist, commenting on the moments after lovemaking.

In the *Portrait of Meyer Schapiro* (1977), Segal lovingly alludes to what he had learned about Cézanne from the scholar by covering the body and back plane with blue. In *Street Meeting* of 1977, his use of color creates atmosphere while also introducing an interesting formal idea. Three people stand together in front of a boarded-up storefront. Had this been a work of the 1960s, one might think they were neighbors idly chatting. But since the dark

84

85

109

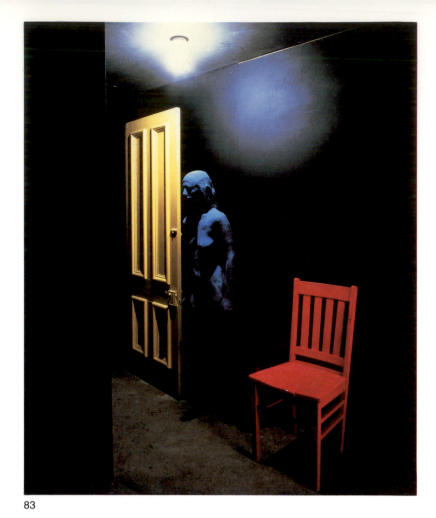

83

83. *The Corridor*, 1976
Plaster, wood, and incandescent light,
84 x 84 x 48 in.
Tamayo Museum, Mexico City

84. *Blue Girl on Black Bed*, 1976
Painted plaster and wood, 44 x 82 x 60 in.
Sydney and Frances Lewis Collection,
Richmond, Virginia

85. *Portrait of Meyer Schapiro*, 1977
Painted plaster, 37⅞ x 26 x 12 in.
The Metropolitan Museum of Art, New York
Gift of Paul Jenkins

84

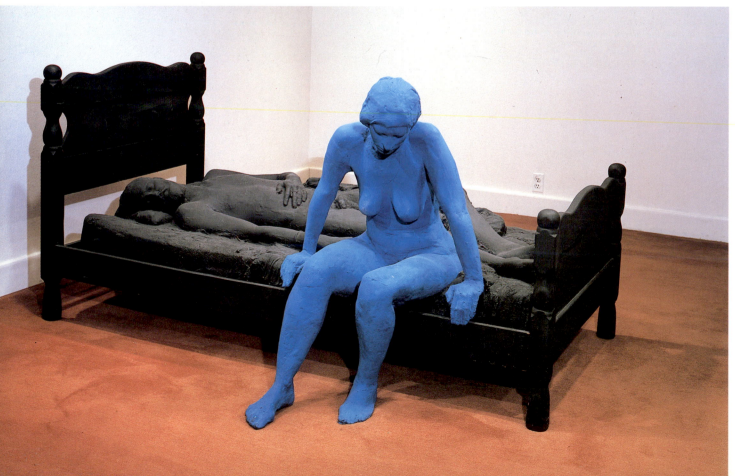

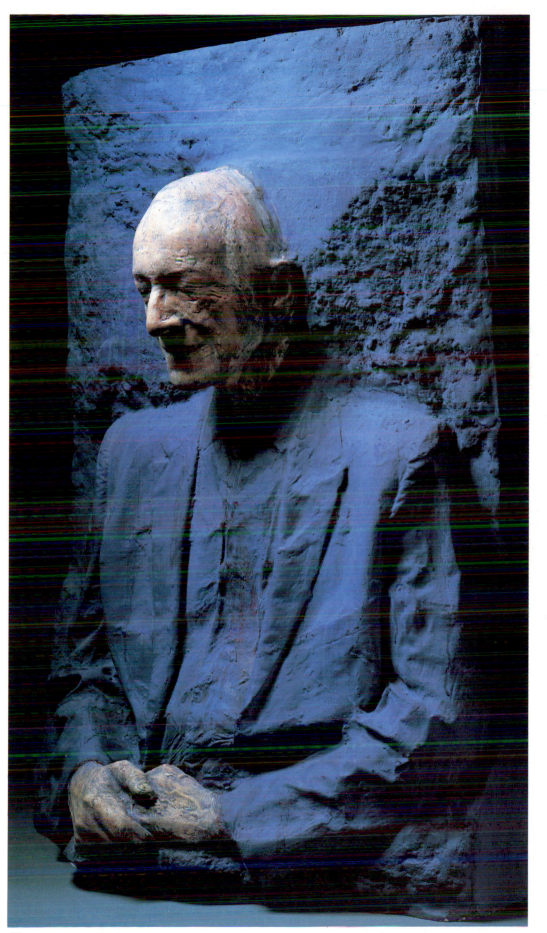

bodies are huddled against an ominous black backdrop their meeting projects a conspiratorial character.

When Segal first began to make sculpture, he found that he could not reuse and reinterpret his themes as freely as he had been able to do in his canvases. Once he began to cover his cast forms with paint, however, he could work with a serial format more easily. Color provided all the change that was necessary. Pose and stance hardly had to be modified. This is particularly clear in a series of works where women stand clothed in front of doorways

86

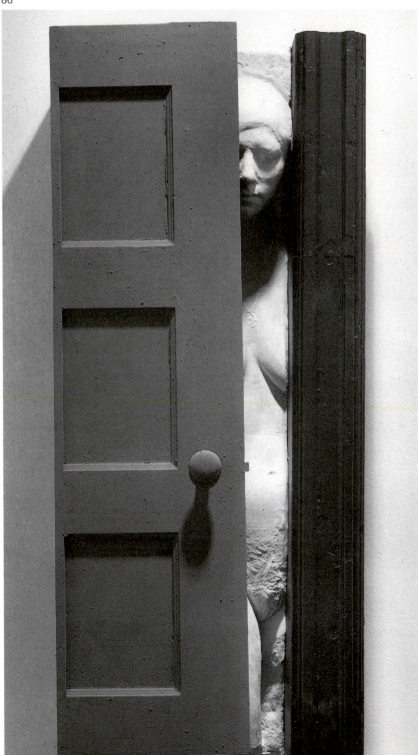

86. *The Blue Door*, 1975
Plaster, wood, and metal, 47 x 19½ x 12½ in.
Courtesy Sidney Janis Gallery, New York

87. Installation view of *An Exhibition of Painted Sculpture*, Sidney Janis Gallery, New York, April 1982

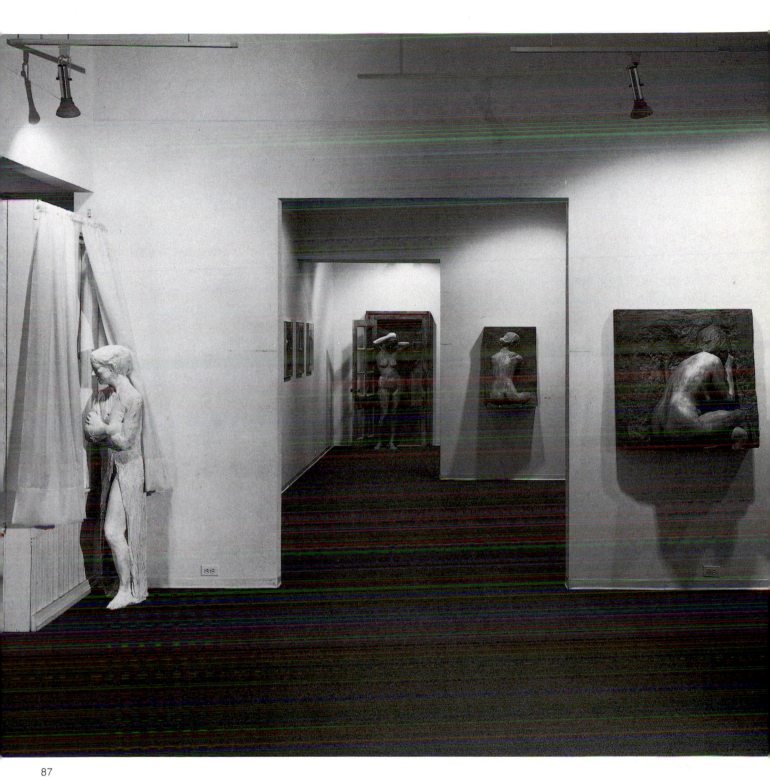

87

and unclothed behind open doors: *Red Girl behind Red Door* (1976), *Blue Girl in Front of Black Doorway* (1977), and *Black Girl, Blue Wall, Red Door* (1978). ⁸⁸

When figure and portal remain constant while color does not, it is obvious that the changing of hue and value totally transforms mood and meaning. These sculptures function like tone poems. Segal might be said to be embodying such phrases as "rosy disposition" or "blue funk" or "black mood."

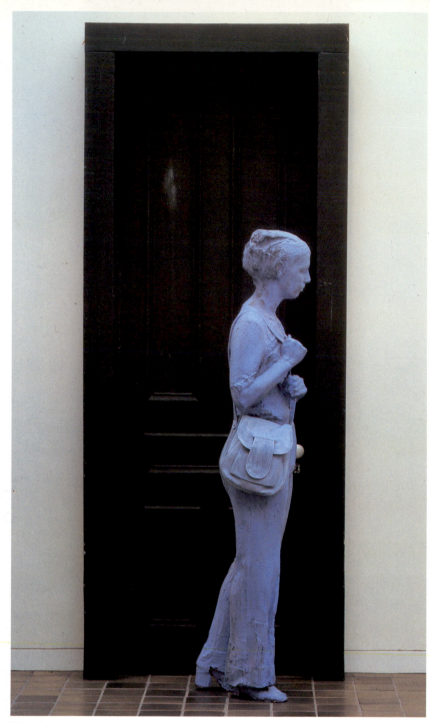

88

In 1981 the suite of works with painted figures and doorways
89 culminated with *Woman Standing in Blue Doorway*, a work that
encapsulates Segal's entire career. Through the door, one glimpses
a room painted in perspective in the style of Segal's canvases of the
1950s. The blue that covers all the other wood surfaces is monochromatic, but sloppily painted, with drips and smudges that never
would have been seen in Segal's work of the 1960s. The woman
is flesh-colored enough to convince us of her naturalness, but her
body and head also carry blues and pinks. If the artist ever made
a three-dimensional painting, this is it. Only the future will tell
whether this sculpture represents a summation or a new beginning.

88. *Blue Girl in Front of Black Doorway*, 1977
Painted plaster, wood, and metal, 98 x 37 x
32 in.
Mr. and Mrs. Leonard Luria, Miami, Florida

89. *Woman Standing in Blue Doorway*, 1981
Painted plaster and wood, 82 x 55 x 33 in.
Collection of the artist

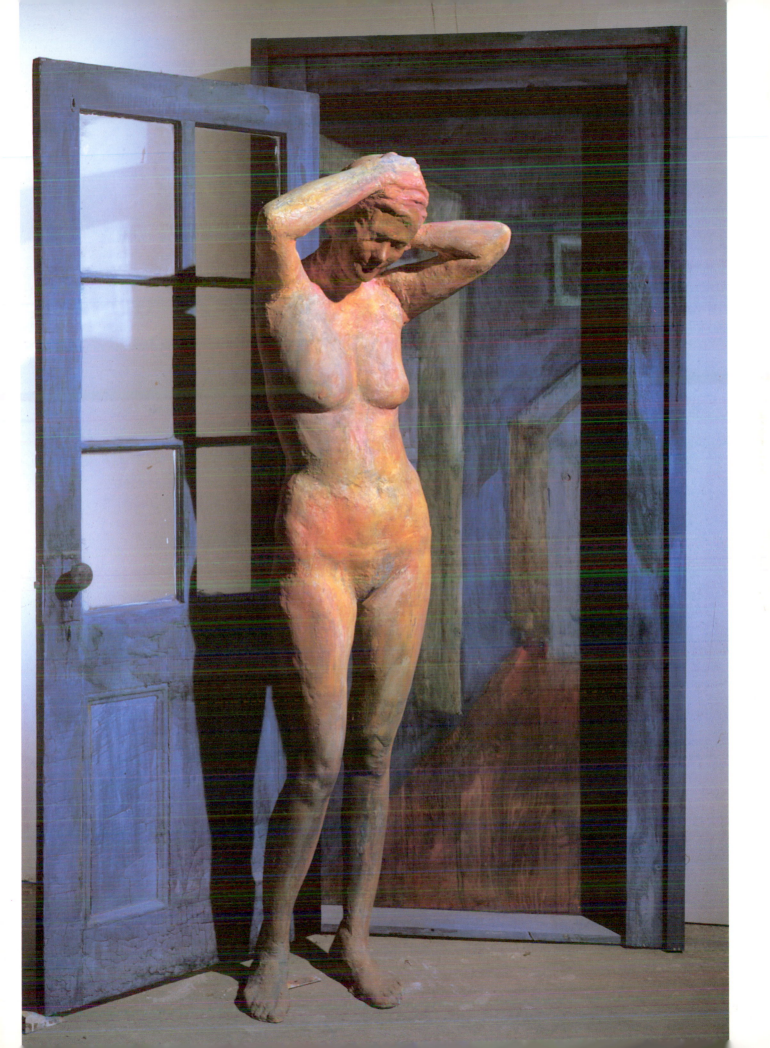

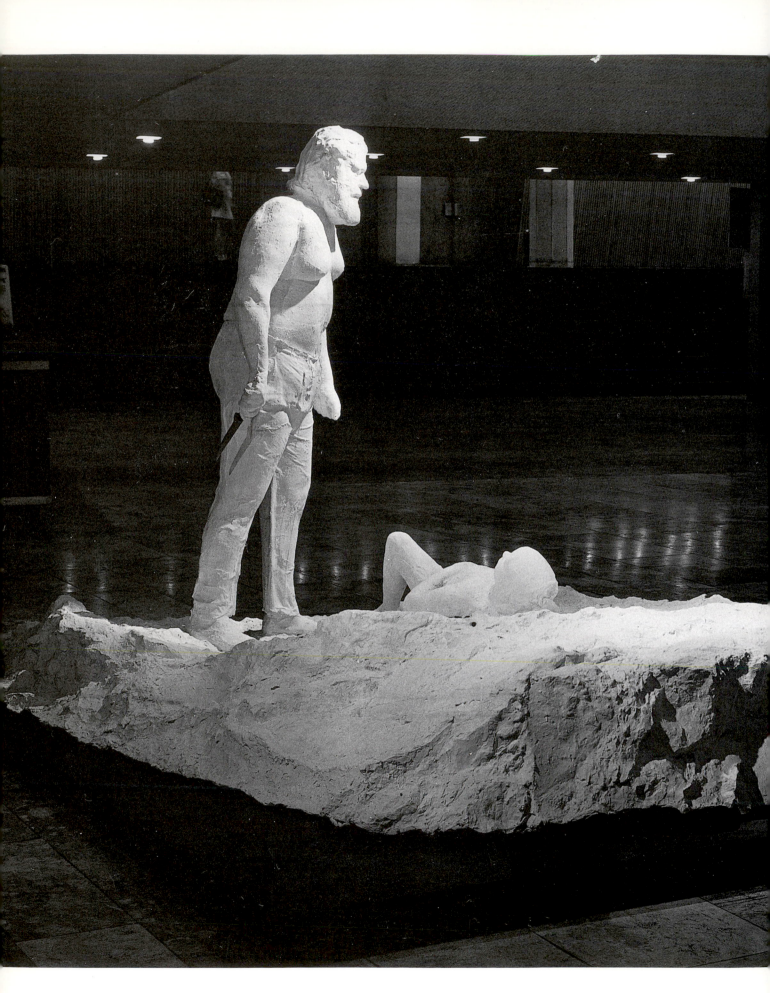

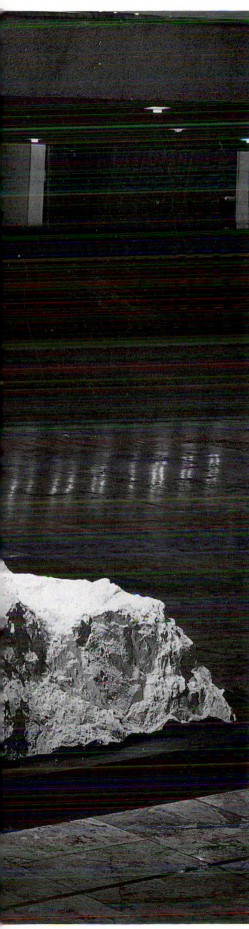

5 Public Commissions

Segal was first asked to make a sculpture for a public site in 1973 by an Israeli foundation. Three years later, residents of Greenwich, Connecticut, sponsored the casting of the artist's first bronze. Also in 1976, the Government Services Administration commissioned an environment for the Federal Building Plaza in Buffalo. A private foundation in 1978 had Segal design a monument to commemorate the demonstrators killed during an antiwar rally at Kent State. That year, too, he met with three other figurative sculptors to discuss work that they would create for a park in Washington, D.C., to serve as a memorial to Franklin Delano Roosevelt. Since then, Segal has executed bronzes for the Port Authority Terminal in New York; a courthouse in Cleveland; a square in Youngstown, Ohio; the museum in Newark, New Jersey; a park in New York's Greenwich Village; and a site overlooking the Golden Gate Bridge in San Francisco. The editors of *Time* magazine had the artist render late in 1982 a scene with computers honoring the "Machine of the Year."

For these projects Segal has treated themes both large and intimate. He has executed works based on the Bible (two versions of the Sacrifice of Isaac) and on historical and political subjects ranging from the Depression to Gay Liberation to the Holocaust. He has dealt, too, with scenes not ordinarily encountered in civic monuments: a restaurant; three commuters; a man in a tollbooth; and steelmakers. Naturalism prevails, a concomitant of his process of casting from life. The bronzes covered with a white patina perfected for Segal's use uncannily resemble the original plaster casts.

Making public commissions has not been easy for Segal. He has had to adjust to new technical problems. Having been trained as a painter, he knew little about bronze. Working in the privacy of his own studio, he had hardly ever begun a sculpture with a specific public site in mind. He also had to learn how to deal with committees, especially those that expected one thing from him and got another. For example, when the Tel Aviv Foundation for Literature and Art approached him in 1973, they had a preconceived image of what he would execute; he had a different idea in mind.

"I think," Segal said not too long ago, "they were looking for a

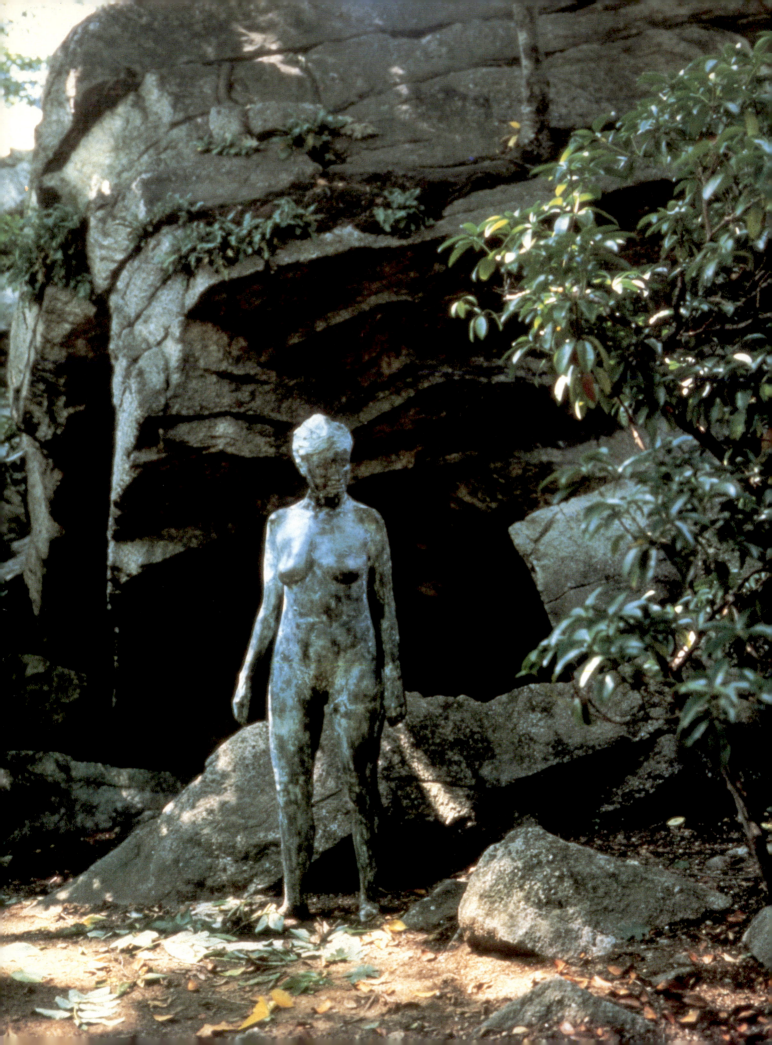

nocturnal, possibly alienated, industrial slum typical of my work." Instead, he chose to deal with Jewish subject matter: the episode in the Torah that is read in temple at the opening of every new year. He executed a *Sacrifice of Isaac*, which met with a storm of protest in a country whose sons and daughters are regularly drafted into the armed forces. Isaac lies on a rocky terrain while Abraham, burly and bearded, towers over his son, a knife clenched in his right fist.

As Segal recalled in 1980, "I got a request to make a sculpture and donate it to the state of Israel. I said yes. Two weeks before I got to Israel, I get a fat letter asking for my plans, drawings, blueprints, complete specs, because it has to be passed by a committee. I sent them a light, jocular letter to the effect that I never do that, I don't make plans, I don't work it all out, but the title is *Abraham and Isaac*. I got a telegram: Either change the subject or change the site . . . I was furious. They were censoring me before I'd even started. Then I got a second telegram, saying it was O.K., come and do what you want, where you want. I discovered that Abba Eban's wife had heard about it, was horrified at the censorship, and read them the riot act. I did the piece, but it never got publicized; it was consigned to a basement somewhere. I put my spies to work and found that the Israelis were reading the piece as a criticism of Zionism, as saying that Israel was sending its sons out to war, out to die. I don't want single-handed, single-level art. I work very hard to pack in a lot of levels. Those bureaucrats weren't willing to read the piece as a detached philosophic examination—they were interpreting it on the simplest political level."[50] Today, Segal still believes that his sculpture is hidden somewhere in the recesses of the Mann Auditorium in Tel Aviv rather than on view in a more public room there.

When asked in 1976 to make his first bronze for a site of his choosing in Greenwich, Connecticut, Segal decided to execute a public sculpture about private experience. *Girl in Nature* is practically hidden in a woody, rock-filled nook of Bruce Park, close to the New England Thruway. At first, the slender, unclothed girl, her hands at her sides, her face turned to her left, looks like a statue taken off a museum pedestal. Her nudity is not the sort generally encountered in an outdoor, public situation. Because avant-garde artists had only just started to work in foundries again, and new patinas had not yet been developed, the figure was covered with a traditional green slip. There is hardly a trace of her ever having been cast in plaster. Nevertheless, *Girl in Nature* is very much an identifiable Segal because the sheltering rock establishes the environmental aspect of the work. Like a denizen of a forest, the figure blends into the scenery so that one mistakenly forgets that the cove is part of the tableau. It is this integration of life with art that separates *Girl in Nature* from comparable statues by Rodin, Maillol, Lehmbruck, and Lachaise even more than the stylization by the older masters of surfaces and anatomies.

Context is also an important factor in *The Restaurant* (1976).[51] Three bronze figures flank a brick wall installed on the side of a government building in Buffalo. Seen against the façade of a modular building where each floor is the same, Segal's work seeks to

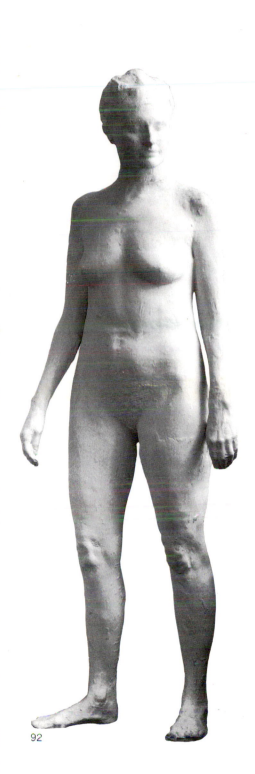

92

90.   *The Sacrifice of Isaac*, 1973 (pp. 88–89)
Plaster, 84 x 108 x 102 in.
Mann Auditorium, Tel Aviv
Donated by the Tel Aviv Foundation for
Literature and Art to the City of Tel Aviv-Yafo

91.   *Girl in Nature*, 1976
Bronze, height: 67 in.
City of Greenwich, Connecticut

92.   *Girl in Nature*, 1976
Plaster, height: 67 in.
Courtesy Sidney Janis Gallery, New York

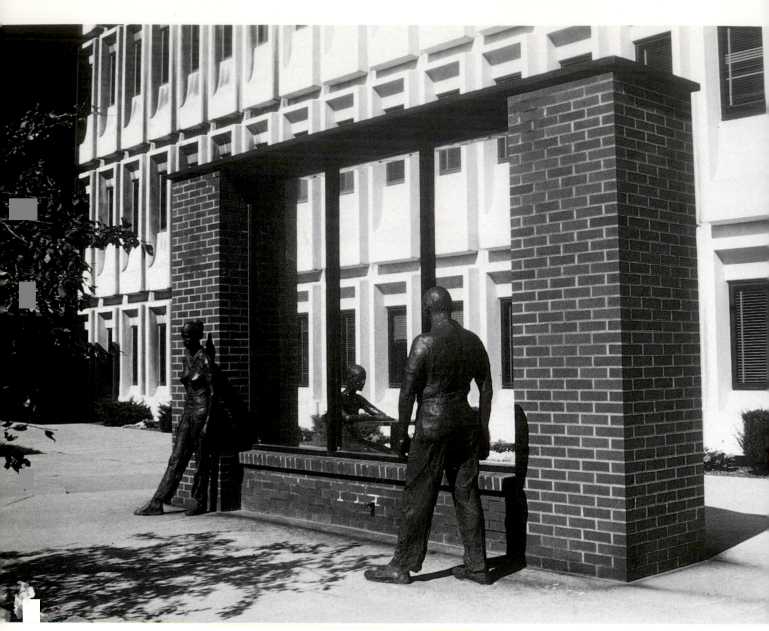

93

restore intimacy to the Federal Building Plaza. Human dimension is brought to an inhumane setting. The storefront is only ten feet high; the characters are life-size. On a warm, sunny day with men and women moving along the plaza or eating their brownbag lunches or simply people-watching, the sculpture echoes the activity swirling around it. On a blustery Sunday in the winter, when the plaza is deserted, the sculpture is a disappointment. Without any animation surrounding the work and lending it meaning, it looks like any other monument plopped down in a public space. Also, the bronze figures, surfaced with a dark patina that hides any evidence of their having once been plaster molds, distance the viewer from the environment because they seem consciously artful.

   When Segal first began to work with bronze, he was at the mercy of the state of the art. The mastery he had attained in his painted plasters and fragments of the same period was out of

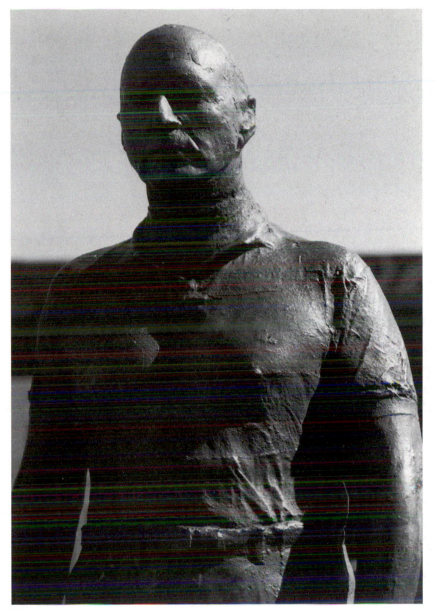

94

reach. For the moment he was more like a young inexperienced artist than an acclaimed sculptor at mid-career. He gained total control of his new medium only when, in 1979, a new durable white patina was perfected in collaboration with technicians at the Johnson Atelier in Princeton. Since light-colored surfaces reveal original textures better than more traditional dark coats, for the first time the plaster-impregnated cloth strips became visible in his bronzes, even though they had always been there.

With *In Memory of May 4, 1970, Kent State: Abraham and Isaac* (1978), Segal reinterpreted his tableau of five years earlier. Another furor surrounded this version made for donation by a private foundation to Kent State. After it was rejected, the sculpture was given to Princeton University, which installed it near the chapel. "My response," Segal has explained, "was to call attention to a metaphor, that the situation that involved the National Guard

93. *The Restaurant*, 1976
Bronze, brick, and glass, 120 x 192 x 96 in.
Federal Office Building, Buffalo, New York,
G.S.A. Commission

94. *The Restaurant*, detail

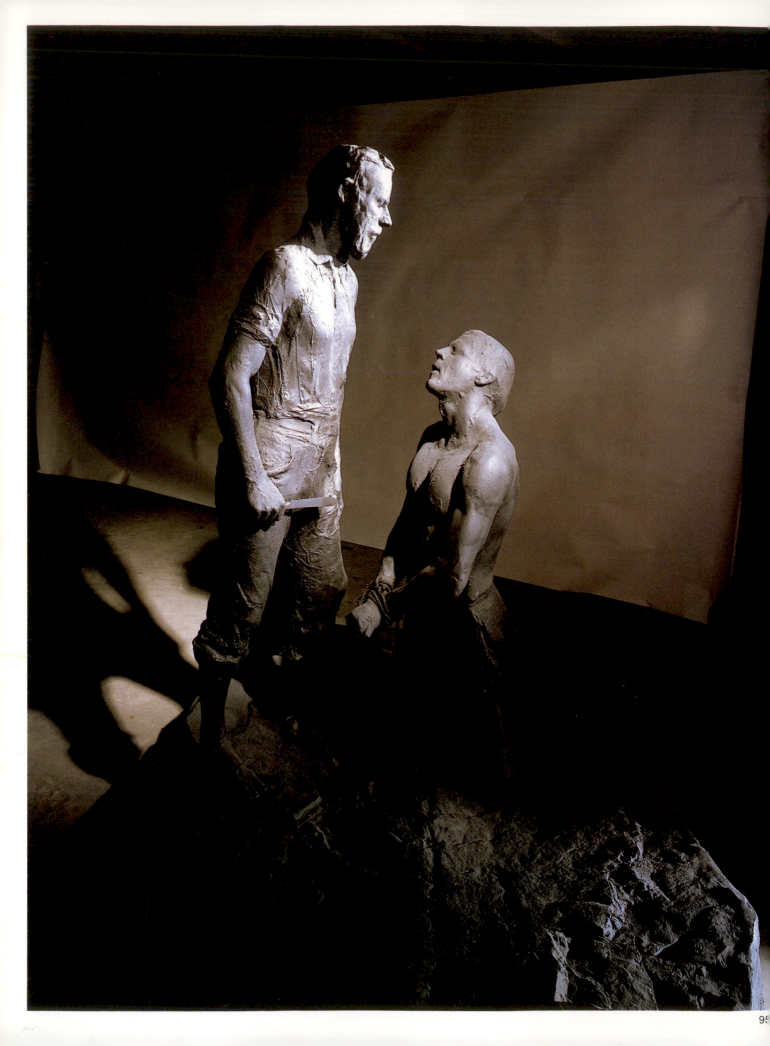

killing students during an antiwar protest was not Right Wing versus Left Wing polemics, but it was more analogous to the Abraham/Isaac terrible, eternal conflict between adherence to an abstract set of principles versus the love for your own child." The artist was later told that he had been expected to cast a National Guardsman having his rifle nudged aside by a naked girl.

About his use of biblical subjects, Segal says he has been drawn to them "because these old stories are so up-to-date." "I don't know if I chose them as religious pieces," he adds. "Everything in our lives, ultimately, is religious in some way." Referring to his works with Abraham and Isaac, he reiterates that they are about "intimate family relationships versus intellectual matters, which is an extremely modern problem."

In 1977 Segal, Robert Graham, Leonard Baskin, and Neil Estern

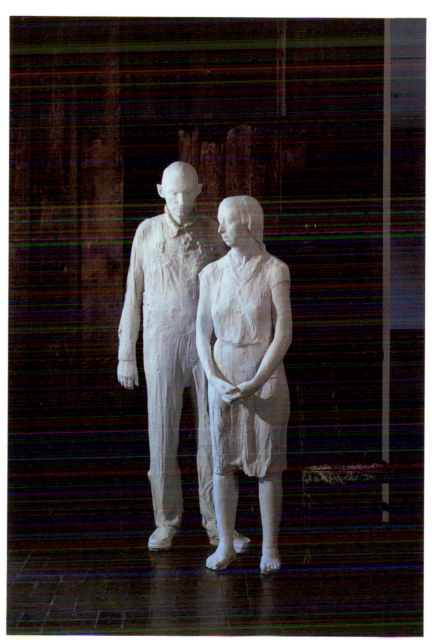

95. *In Memory of May 4, 1970, Kent State: Abraham and Isaac*, 1978
Painted plaster, rope, and metal, 84 x 120 x 50 in.
The John B. Putnam, Jr., Memorial Collection, Princeton University, New Jersey

96. *Appalachian Farm Couple—1936*, 1978
Plaster, wood, metal, and glass, 108 x 90 x 36 in.
Neuberger Museum, State University of New York, College at Purchase

96

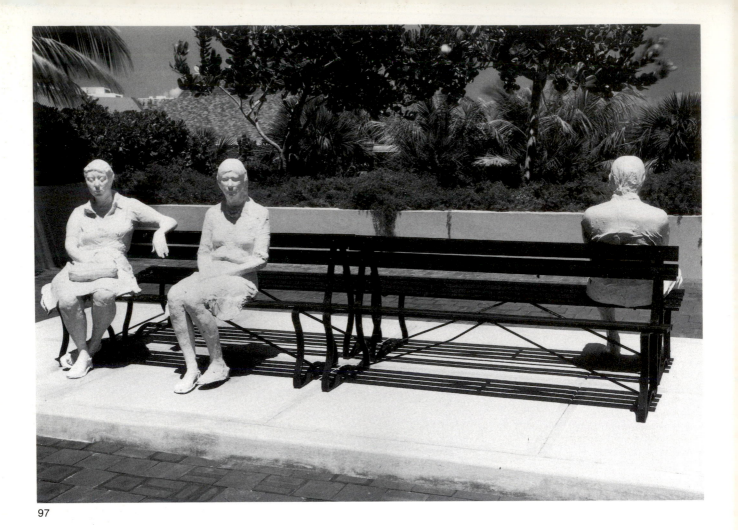

97

were selected to execute sculptures for a park to be designed by landscape architect Lawrence Halprin as a memorial to Franklin Delano Roosevelt. (Both houses of Congress have finally approved the project; President Reagan has signed the bill; as of the summer of 1983, only funds needed to be appropriated.)

During the summer of 1978, while discussing the FDR project, Segal said, "I have a personal prejudice against enormous, impersonal monuments, and I was trying to conceive an approach that can keep human scale, personal feeling, personal intensity."[52] By then, he, like his colleagues, had decided to deal with images that epitomized events of the Depression and World War II. Segal would cast an Appalachian couple standing in front of their cabin; seven figures waiting in a bread line; a fireside-chat scene; a mound of corpses alluding to the horrors of the Holocaust; and possibly an assembly line depicting "the arsenal of democracy."

Before the project was temporarily shelved, Segal cast two gaunt figures—a man in overalls and a simply dressed woman—and constructed the front of a wood cabin with an old chair and a kerosene lamp hanging by the door. Scenes with people in front of architectural backdrops are one of Segal's favorite themes. In this instance, body language and the quiet, grave dignity of the man and woman recall the couple in Grant Wood's *American Gothic* of 1930, although Segal's scene was actually inspired by a photograph taken by Ben Shahn for the Farm Security Administration.

96

97. *Three People on Four Park Benches*, 1980
Bronze and steel, 66 x 144 x 54 in.
Martin Z. Margulies, Miami, Florida

98, 99. *Next Departure*, 1979
Painted bronze with metal and glass, 84 x 72 x 96 in.
Port Authority Terminal, New York

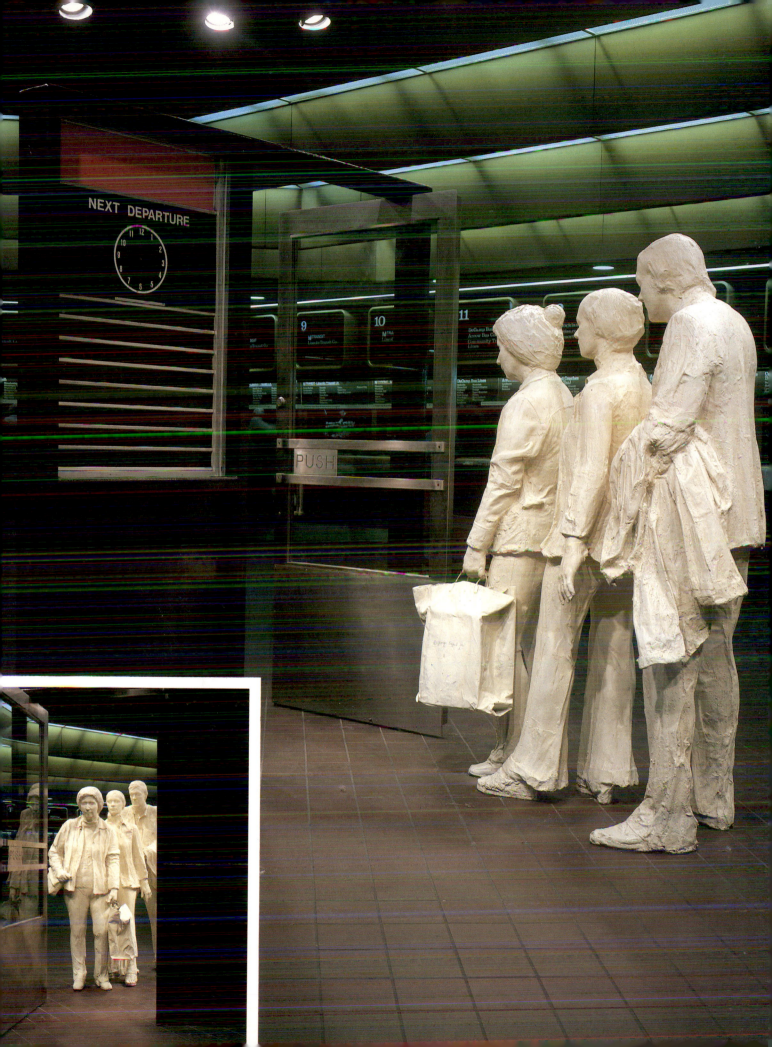

Discussing his participation in the FDR memorial, Segal said, "My history is working on what I feel like. I had to wrestle with myself about suddenly dropping my mode of working to satisfy a public commission." He added, "I wouldn't want that mass audience if I had to sacrifice the density of my statement—that's what the hard work has been about."[53]

Two bronze commissions that Segal worked on in 1979—*Three People on Four Park Benches* for the Cuyahoga County Justice Center in Cleveland and *Next Departure* for the Port Authority Terminal in Manhattan (installed 1982)—have proven to be among his most popular works and also among his most successful aesthetic accomplishments. Both are equally effective when viewed from either of two directions. In the former, two women and one man sit on two sets of benches placed back-to-back. In the latter, two women and a man wait for a bus by the open door of a departure gate. Although no clock ticks and nothing moves, each sculpture vividly conveys the passing of time.

Three People on Four Park Benches, stretching twelve feet in length, displays the same kind of lateral spread that Segal had utilized in *The Gas Station* of 1964. Horizontality is emphasized further by the linearity of the benches. There is obviously plenty of room for a viewer to sit down with this trio of idlers.

Viewer identification and involvement also characterizes *Next Departure*. One feels like collecting tickets from these enervated travelers when they are seen head-on through the open door. One feels like joining the queue when they are glimpsed from the rear. By offering such strong participatory sensations—from two directions, no less—*Next Departure* (which incorporates the same kind of gate one passes through on bus trips to the artist's home) offers a literal, not just a fictive, identification with the characters. People in the Port Authority Terminal are often seen taking photographs of their companions standing in line with the bronze commuters.

Since a viewer can stand in front of or behind the commuters, Segal avoids the pictorial or the bas-relief nature of many of his other works with architectural features. A master like Giotto, for example, in the fourteenth-century fresco cycle in the Arena Chapel in Padua, often placed the back of a figure toward the viewer, and it was over the shoulder of such a character that one regarded the scene and felt a part of it. In *Next Departure*, one looks in both directions, front and rear. These are the primary viewing points, but there are other interesting angles as well. From the sides, the two women and the man have been set in a stepped arrangement. The angle of a stooped shoulder, the way a handbag is held so that it can not be snatched by a mugger are details one can easily relate to. *Three People on Four Park Benches* and *Next Departure* both convincingly portray situations in which we might readily find ourselves.

In 1980 Segal executed *The Steelmakers*, measuring 216 by 240 by 180 inches and incorporating sixty-five tons of steel. Two foundry operators, wearing goggles and hard hats, are about to heat some metal in a crucible that would, if this were real life, be part of a huge furnace (the one seen here was retrieved from a shutdown mill). The bronze figures are covered with a dark patina that not

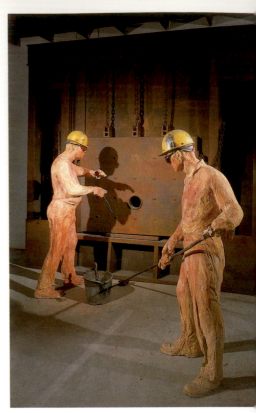

100

100. *The Steelmakers*, 1980
Painted plaster, wood, plastic, and metal, 120 x 120 x 60 in.
Courtesy Sidney Janis Gallery, New York

101. *The Steelmakers*, 1980
Bronze, steel, and painted plastic, 216 x 240 x 180 in.
City of Youngstown, Ohio
Commissioned by the Youngstown Area Arts Council with the support of the National Endowment for the Arts, the Ohio Arts Council, and public subscription

102. *Gay Liberation*, detail. See plate 103

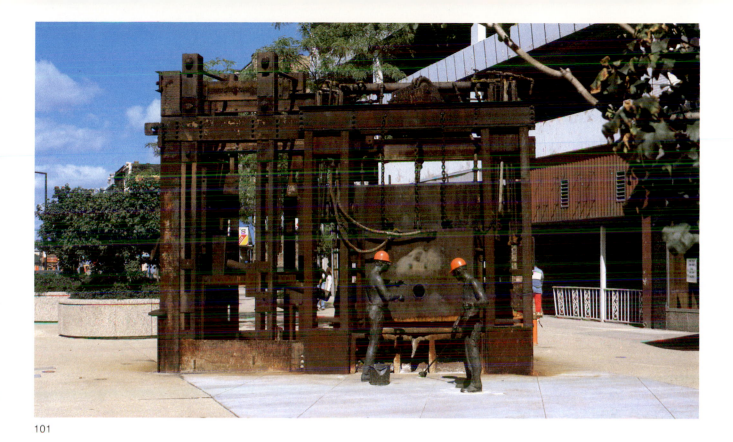

101

102

only blends with the equipment but calls to mind as well the way mill hands emerge dirty from a hard day's work. Commissioned by Youngstown, Ohio, for placement in a city square, the sculpture celebrates the principal industry of a town currently plagued by one of the highest unemployment rates in the United States.

In 1980 Segal executed another commission for the Mildred Andrews Fund, the foundation that had earlier sponsored the project for Kent State. This was *Gay Liberation*, to be placed in Greenwich Village's Christopher Park, at Sheridan Square, near the site of the riot of 1969 that helped give birth to this movement. On one of two park benches, two women sit close to one another; one touches the left thigh of her companion, who responds by lightly placing her right hand atop her friend's gesture. Near them, two men clad in tight jeans stand together, the left arm of one resting against the other's shoulder.

Never one to shy away from difficult subject matter, Segal accepted the commission for *Gay Liberation* after the homosexual artist who had originally been approached to make the sculpture backed out of the project at the urging of her gallery. (A trustee of the Mildred Andrews Fund has related that Segal subsequently became second, third, and fourth choice for the project.) Lovers have been a recurring theme in Segal's oeuvre. Encountered in doorways, bedrooms, and even motels, kissing, caressing, and before, during, and after lovemaking, amorous couples were cast as stark, white plasters during the 1960s and as painted figures during the 1970s. In 1969 two lesbian friends of the artist were cast as *The Girlfriends*.

Though Segal delicately treated a theme that could have been harsh and strident—he might, for example, have depicted some

103

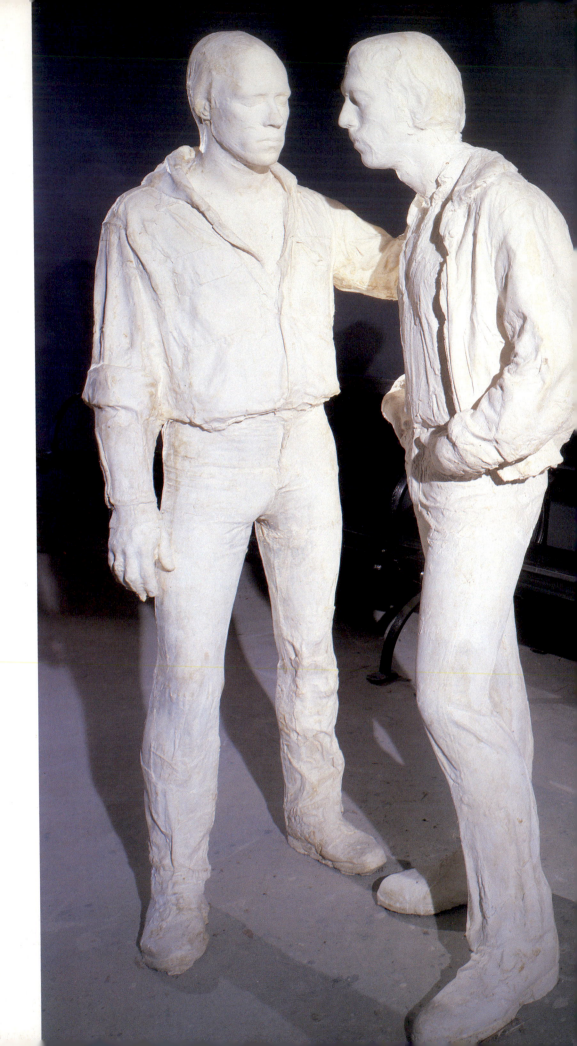

103. *Gay Liberation*, 1980
Plaster and metal, 71 x 192 x 80 in.
Courtesy Sidney Janis Gallery, New York

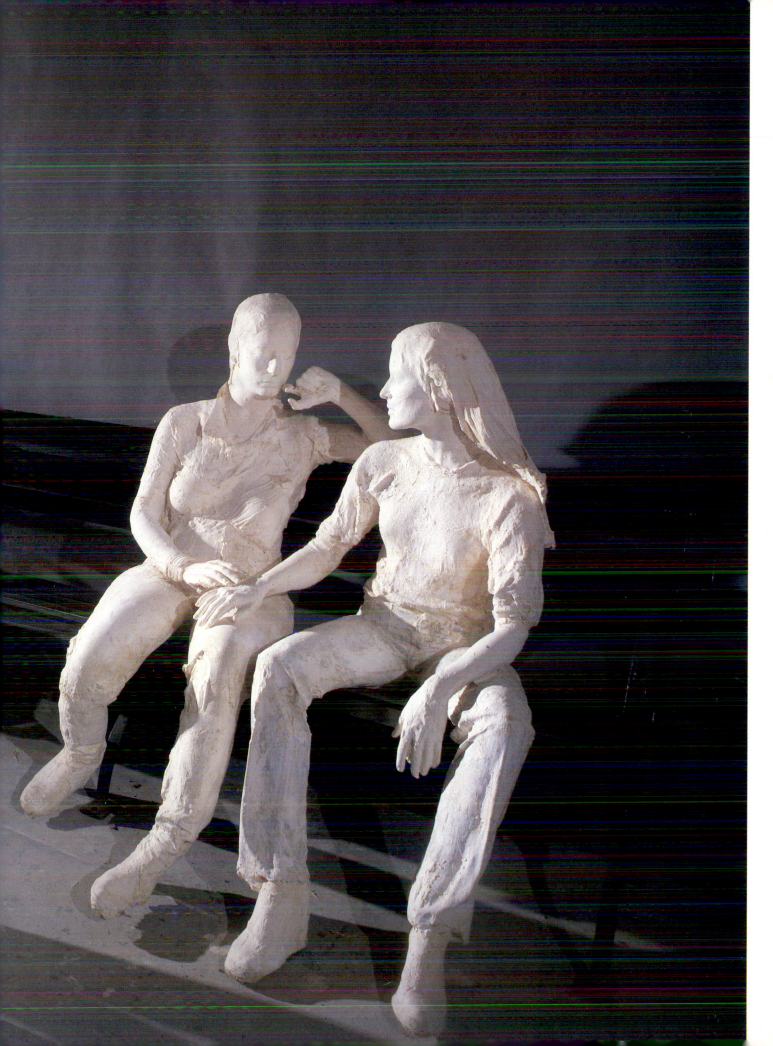

aspect of the 1969 riot or portrayed a caricature of homosexual love—he was pounced on by straights and gays alike, and the matter remains unresolved. Heterosexuals in the neighborhood did not want to daily see a monument to Gay Liberation. Homosexual activists had different expectations—some, for example, were disappointed that two young white couples were cast rather than older or racially mixed pairs. Segal was perplexed. "If I make a statement in relation to the political aspects of homosexuality, if my statement simply put, says, 'Gays are human comma too,' that mild statement seems to be enough to open a Pandora's box of theory and confrontation."

After being asked why controversy has surrounded some commissions and not others, Segal commented, "It's been fashionable for more than a decade to be critical of the museum/gallery scene as examples of establishment corruption and domination. On the contrary, I've been discovering that the gallery/museum situation for an artist is the last refuge for free expression along with public libraries. Just as libraries will collect the best of literature and there are no X and R ratings involved with books you borrow, so with museums and galleries as far as literary content goes in the art work."

Each commission that Segal has completed has reached a different constituency. The January 3, 1983, issue of *Time* magazine is a case in point. For the cover heralding the "Machine of the Year," the artist cast in plaster a family of three (husband, wife, daughter —only the child was not photographed for the fold-out) accompanied by two computers, colored chairs and tables, and a window, all viewed against a wood floor and a black wall. The environment was seen not only by millions of subscribers and newsstand browsers, it was broadcast over countless nightly news programs. The artist could not have reached a wider audience nor been more delighted by the reactions he provoked. He found a great deal of pleasure working with the editors of *Time* in a commercial art situation more than three and a half decades after having decided to become a fine artist.

To produce the "Machine of the Year" cover, Segal momentarily interrupted a project that had engaged his attention since the spring of 1982. For a competition sponsored by Mayor Diane Feinstein's Committee for a Memorial to the Six Million Victims of the Holocaust, he had been developing a work that, if selected, would be cast in bronze. His sculpture has been chosen, and it will be installed in Lincoln Park, overlooking Golden Gate Bridge in San Francisco.

To get himself started, Segal went to a Zionist library in Manhattan, which had on file scores of photographs he remembered having seen after the concentration camps were liberated in 1945. "We stack cans in our grocery stores with more order and love than the way the Germans dumped these bodies," he has said.[54] In his sculpture, ten emaciated corpses, nude and partially clothed, are splayed across the ground in a pinwheel configuration behind a barbed-wire fence where a lone survivor stands facing viewers. When seen in person, each individual form has impact. When seen in reproduction, the work reverts to the horrific nature of the

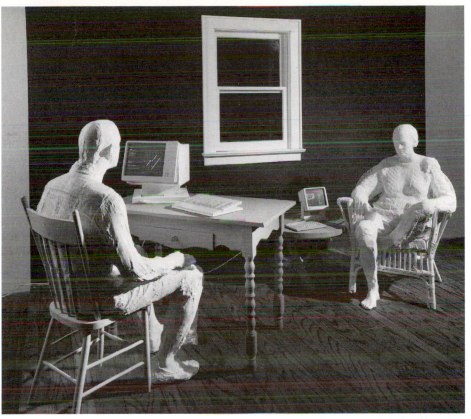

104

scenes that inspired it: it presents itself as a mass of corpses haphazardly piled together.

The composition of fence and survivor was also guided by a photograph, one taken by Margaret Bourke-White, and the man who posed was an Israeli friend of the artist's who had indeed walked out of a camp. Segal had immediately turned to these sources because he had been ruminating upon this project for years. For the FDR Memorial, he had originally considered doing a heap of bodies, and sculptor Leonard Baskin was going to render a scene based on the Bourke-White photograph. When invited to participate in the Holocaust competition, Segal turned to these images because the FDR Memorial had been put aside for quite some time. Segal had not anticipated being depressed by the project, but during the months that he was surrounded by images of deaths and disorders, the plaster corpses in his studio dragged his spirits down.

Unless sources in the sculpture are pointed out, they are not apparent. This is true of many of the bronze works. Ironically, naturalism prevails in the public commissions even more than it had in the plaster sculptures of the 1960s. In the earlier works, one more readily recognized motifs borrowed from art history. Later on, mood and meaning predominate. Still, once the array of individuals in Segal's Holocaust memorial has been studied, other levels do emerge. Like *The Execution*, in which references to Mussolini's public humiliation and to Masaccio's *Martyrdom of St. Peter* were incorporated, the monument for San Francisco reveals deeper concerns. Segal introduced religious allegory into this work. A woman holding a partially chewed apple lies across the rib of a

104. *Machine of the Year*, 1982
Plaster, wood, plastic, mixed media, 120 x 144 x 84 in.
Time, Inc., New York

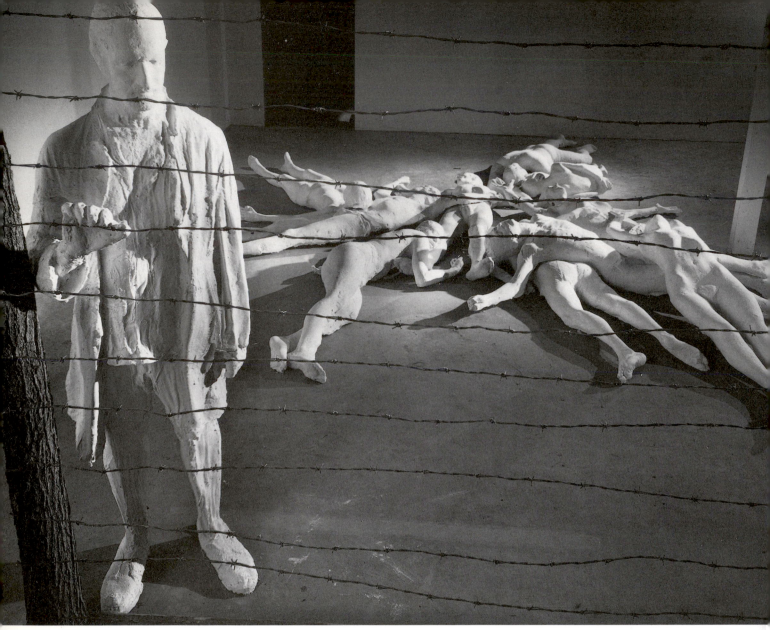

105

man. Together, they refer to Adam and Eve. An older man who has fallen beside a young boy calls to mind Abraham and Isaac. Another man with outstretched arms suggests a crucified Christ. Thus, Segal once again seems to have drawn comparisons, as he did in *The Legend of Lot* and the two versions of the Sacrifice of Isaac, between the lives of humble, contemporary folk and Old Testament predecessors. In this instance, though, instead of confronting biblical characters first and then drawing parallels with modern philosophical issues, the viewer relates first to contemporaries who allude to religious figures.

Civic commissions have allowed Segal to make private statements in a public forum. As a figurative artist, he has achieved what he had been seeking to express during the 1950s in his semi-abstract canvases. His expressionism now has a purpose. He has wedded the ethos of Abstract Expressionism to realistic images imbued with meaning. The jumble of corpses in the Holocaust memorial can be compared to the kind of slash marks popular

105. *The Holocaust*, 1982
Plaster, wood, and wire, 120 x 240 x 240 in.
Courtesy Sidney Janis Gallery, New York

106. *The Holocaust*, detail

with some members of the New York School. Thus, these bodies are expressive formally as well as morally.

Exceptional attendance figures were recorded by the Jewish Museum when the plaster version of the Holocaust Memorial was exhibited during the spring of 1983. The crowd that flocked to the museum faced the work of an artist who had attained the mix of form and meaning he had long strived for. And it was more than fitting that Segal had this project placed on view for the first time in the institution that had given his career its initial boost in 1957. His past and present, his tentative gropings as a painter, and his mastery as a sculptor were joined together.

During the summer of 1981, Segal said, "I would hate to be kicked upstairs to become the servant to illustrate the attitudes of wealthy patrons." The twelve commissions he has already executed seem to have proved that he need not fear this ever occurring.

George Segal has refused to let his accumulating fame affect the development of his art. In the privacy of his studio, he ignores the constantly ringing telephone, the piles of letters requesting information, loans, and speaking engagements, and the dealers who suggest he make new works that look like earlier popular sculptures. He has not only altered the procedures he initially used to cast friends, relatives, and models, but has expanded his vocabulary as well to encompass the production of more costly bronzes for outdoor sites. When everyone said a typical Segal was a walk-in environment, he started making anatomical fragments that could hang on walls and sit on pedestals. When everyone said white plasters were the hallmark of his style, he began painting their surfaces. Themes he first treated in the mid-1960s still engage his attention; but they have evolved so that pose and object have not been merely reshuffled. During the past two decades, his varied body of work has gone in directions that never could have been anticipated in 1961 when he stoically sat for his first sculpture.

One constant remains in Segal's art: the basic criteria for evaluating a completed work. "The final piece accumulates on many levels answering twelve questions simultaneously," he once explained. "How does it hit me esthetically? How true is it psychologically? How many levels and conflicts are revealed by space and encounter?"[55] For Segal, these are practically Talmudic matters. They reflect discussions about form and meaning he had with Allan Kaprow during the 1950s when both were seeking to transcend the strictures of modernism embodied in Abstract Expressionism. They also reflect discussions about the nature of Old Master paintings he had with Meyer Schapiro when the young artist and the scholar met in the back room of the Hansa Gallery.

Segal's audience consists of many different constituencies. No one can say whether the general public recognizes all the complexities of Segal's work but to some they obviously respond. The art world has showered his work with all the glories young artists dream of: museum retrospectives, books, documentary films. The academic community invites him to speak at their universities and confers honors upon him. His sculpture turns up in unlikely places. *Gottlieb's Wishing Well* appeared in the Italian film *The Tenth Victim*. The plot of *Games*, a 1967 Hollywood movie, centered on

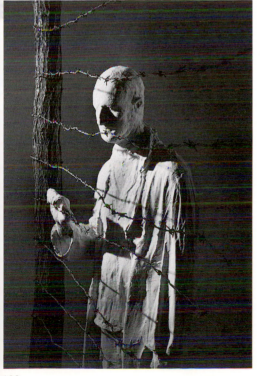

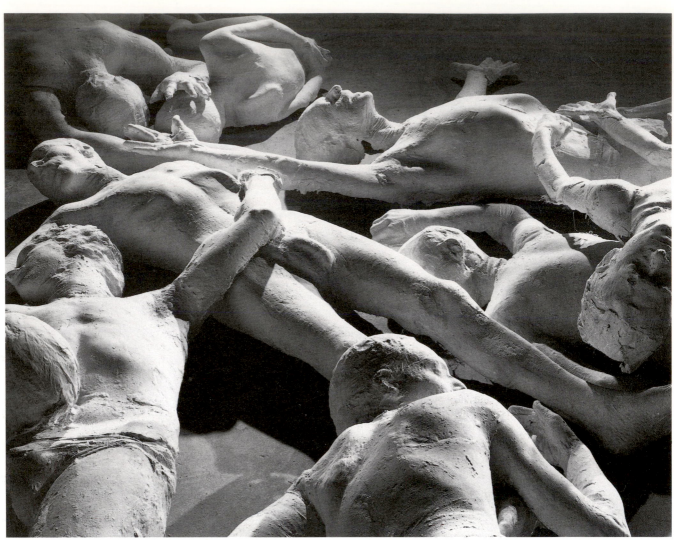

107

a corpse hidden in a hollow plaster figure that imitated his art, while the loft apartment of a hi-tech architect in Paul Mazursky's *Tempest* was decorated with one of his reliefs. Anne Beattie used Segal's Whitney retrospective as a leitmotif in her novel *Falling in Place*. An advertising campaign based on the slogan, "When you come in a Van Heusen shirt the rest come off like a bunch of stiffs" was illustrated with ersatz Segal casts.

Yet, with all the fuss that has been made about his art, Segal remains a humble, family man. Once he settled in New Jersey, he never moved. The chicken coops he built on his farm continue to serve as his sculpture studio. In New York, three galleries have handled his work—he left the first two only after they ceased to operate. With the exception of his travels around the globe to install his sculptures, his simple lifestyle has hardly changed.

In 1963 Segal mentioned how, when he was painting 6-foot-by-8-foot canvases, his wife, a forthright, down-to-earth woman, would suggest he make smaller pictures that would sell more readily. "I would answer, 'What difference does it make since I don't sell work in any style?' My wife was exasperated. 'If you can't sell the

107. *The Holocaust*, detail. See plate 105

large paintings, how will you be able to sell those enormous sculptures?' That wasn't important to me since I never imagined that my art could sell."[56]

Not too long ago, Segal echoed the sentiments he expressed two decades ago. When asked if he was doing what he might have imagined for himself had he looked into the future thirty years ago, he replied, "When I went into art, there was no history of an American artist making a living at it. Not in fine arts. Commercial arts, yes. If you wanted to do exactly your own thing, you couldn't expect anybody to buy it. You might be supporting yourself at some other job, and eating and drinking with fellow artists." A smile beamed across his gentle face after he said this. We are his subjects, and he is his own man.

NOTES

1. Quoted in David Patrick Stearns, "Cheers and Jeers for Public 'Works,'" *USA Today*, March 8, 1983, p. 2D.

2. George Segal, "Commentaries on Six Sculptures," p. 41.

3. Unless otherwise indicated, this and all subsequent quotes come from conversations the author has had with the artist and others during the past two years.

4. Leo Steinberg, exhibition review, *Arts Magazine* 30 (April 1956): 44–45.

5. Ibid., p. 45.

6. Barbara Guest, exhibition review, *Arts Magazine* 30 (March 1956): 60.

7. Leo Steinberg, "Introduction," in Meyer Schapiro, *The New York School: Second Generation*, p. 5.

8. Elizabeth Pollet, exhibition review, *Arts Magazine* 31 (May 1957): 50.

9. Parker Tyler, exhibition review, *Artnews* 56 (May 1957): 12.

10. R. Warren Dash, exhibition review, *Arts Magazine* 32 (February 1958): 57.

11. Phyllis Tuchman, "Interview with George Segal," pp. 74–75.

12. George Segal, "Perspectives of American Sculpture," p. 147.

13. Sidney Tillim, exhibition review, *Arts Magazine* 33 (February 1959): 57.

14. James Schuyler, exhibition review, *Artnews* 57 (February 1959): 16.

15. Quoted in "The Silent People," p. 107.

16. Caption in Brydon Smith, *Dine Oldenburg Segal*, exhibition catalog, Toronto: Art Gallery of Ontario, 1967, p. 61.

17. Quoted in Jean Dypréau, "Métamorphoses: L'Ecole de New York," p. 164.

18. "The Found Object: Can It Be Art?" a panel discussion at the Institute of Contemporary Art, Boston, March 7, 1966, unpublished manuscript.

19. Jill Johnston, exhibition review, *Artnews* 61 (May 1962): 16.

20. Tuchman, "Interview," p. 79.

21. "Successful Sculptor Hunts for the Truth," *New Brunswick Home News*, January 14, 1963, n.p.

22. "People Are Talking About . . . George Segal," p. 98.

23. Besides Segal and Kaprow, Roy Lichtenstein, George Brecht, Lucas Samaras, Gary Kuehn, and Robert Whitman have had ties to the state university. Whitman was an English major; others taught in the engineering, history, and physics departments. Samaras was an undergraduate; Kuehn earned an M.F.A. degree. Brecht first met the rest of the group while he was a scientist at the Johnson and Johnson laboratories.

24. Allan Kaprow, *Ten from Rutgers University*, exhibition catalog, New York: Bianchini Gallery, 1965, p. 3.

25. Barbara Rose, "Dada Then and Now," p. 23.

26. Phyllis Tuchman, "POP!" p. 25.

27. The two principal exhibitions that have been devoted to Pop art—one held at the Hayward Gallery in London in 1969 and the other mounted by the Whitney Museum of American Art in 1974—had *Cinema* installed at their entrances.

28. Barbara Rose and Irving Sandler, eds., "Sensibility of the Sixties," p. 55.

29. Segal, "Commentaries," p. 33. Other quotes concerning *Cinema* are from the same source.

30. "People Are Talking About," p. 98.

31. "Plaster Bandage People from the Farm," *Chicago Sun-Times*, April 14, 1968, n.p.

32. Henry Geldzahler, "An Interview with George Segal," p. 27.

33. Segal, "Commentaries," p. 37. Subsequent quotes concerning *The Diner* are from the same source.

34. Segal used silver paint, as he had already done in *The Dry-Cleaning Store* and *Woman in a Doorway, I*. After this work was completed, Chamberlain began using galvanized aluminum in his own sculpture. Consequently, Segal's choice of a gray was not as incompatible in spirit with Chamberlain's art as some other color might have been.

35. Quoted in Jan van der Marck, *George Segal*, 1975, p. 147.

36. Segal, "Commentaries," p. 49.

37. Ibid.

38. Quoted in José L. Barrio-Garay, *George Segal: Environments*, p. 13.

39. Ibid.

40. "The Super Micro-Macro World of Wonderama," *Time* 86 (December 17, 1965): 73.

41. The final painting of the figures—Segal refers to them as "abstract shafts of color"—was affected by his reading *Black Elk Speaks*, a book about the life of an Indian medicine man. Segal, "Commentaries," p. 44.

42. Tuchman, "Interview," p. 77.

43. "The Arts: Protest on All Sides," *Newsweek* 70 (July 10, 1967): 60.

44. Richard Bellamy, "Excerpts from a Conversation," n.p.

45. Ibid.

46. Tuchman, "Interview," p. 79.

47. Hilton Kramer, replying to a question following a lecture at New York University, April 19, 1983.

48. Segal, "Commentaries," p. 49.

49. Ibid.

50. "Sculpture (Cont'd.)," *New Yorker*, p. 44.

51. Segal had worked with lunch counter and diner scenes before, and with the image of a woman seated at a table by a restaurant window twice before. *The Restaurant Window, I*, 1967, includes a man passing along the street outside. In *The Restaurant Window, II*, 1971, a film of a coffee cup was once projected against the window.

52. Malcolm Carter, "The FDR Memorial," p. 56.

53. Ibid.

54. From a talk presented at the Jewish Museum, New York, April 7, 1983.

55. Tuchman, "POP!" p. 25.

56. George Segal, "Statement," Paris, p. 3.

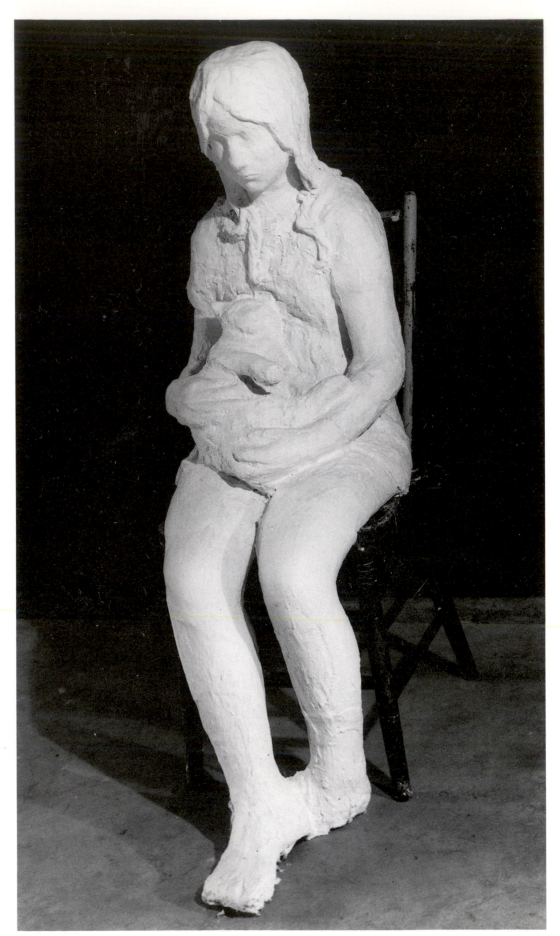

Artist's Statements

The look of these figures is both accidental and planned. I usually know generally what emotional stance I'd like to have in the finished figure and I ask the model to stand or sit in a certain way. That model though is a human being with a great deal of mystery and totality locked up in the figure. In spite of my technique certain truths of bone structure are revealed and so are long time basic attitudes of response on the part of the model. If you have to sit still for an hour you fall into yourself and it is impossible to hide, no matter the stance. . . .

The whiteness intrigues me; for all its special connotations of disembodied spirit, inseparable from the fleshy corporeal details of the figure. Color itself interests me a great deal. In the total compositions I use the built in color of the real objects and increasingly I'm concerned with color as light rather than color as paint.

Henry Geldzahler, "An Interview with George Segal," 1964, pp. 27, 29.

As to my casting, I can tell you that a mystery takes place that I never expected, and it's different each time. The simple act of somebody taking a position and putting pieces of cloth saturated in plaster on them, and having that person sit until sections harden has had a very unexpected side result. I think that's why I continue casting; otherwise I'd have been bored to tears and gone to something else long ago. First of all the wetness shows the muscles and bones underneath the clothing. It saturates the clothes to the point where you can see bone structure underneath. The discomfort to the person is of such a nature that they can't pretend with me; they have to relax, and they're just as stoic and brave, or screaming and hysterical as they really are. It's very hard to be a fake with that kind of wet discomfort over such a long period of time. Maybe I'm a sadist, I don't know. But then I've also done the same person over six or seven times, and I've been absolutely amazed to find that even slight differences in state of mind come through that I can't control in the finished sculpture.

From a lecture delivered at the Albright-Knox Art Gallery, Buffalo, February 28, 1967.

[The fragments will] probably stay as themselves, as independent thoughts or sensations. They provoked a lot of questions for me:

108. *Girl Holding a Cat*, 1968
Plaster and wood, 48 x 17 x 32 in.
Helen Segal

they looked beautiful strewn around on the floor or when I picked them up and handled them and looked at them casually and intimately. What were they: notations? loving comments? lyric statements? glimpses? If I left them on the floor, they were like leaves. If I put them on the wall, they could be a bit out of a Cubist collage. I remember some Cubist paintings as bits and pieces of the real world strewn on a canvas to make a musical harmony. My memory of walking down a city street has to do with the glimpses of things I've seen that stick in my mind.

Richard Bellamy, "Excerpts from a Conversation," 1970 (taped October 13, 1969), n.p.

I find it increasingly difficult to separate abstraction from figuration. If the impulse for a work starts some place in the real world where I've been, or in some reaction I've had inside myself to something outside myself, that's already complicated, and while I'm working everything shuffles back and forth. It's a real person, a real gesture, real places, real things. If I'm going to come anywhere close to the essence of experience, I'll suppress extraneous detail. I'll change color; I'll carve space. I can't violate truth about the person, his body build, his characteristic attitudes. I can't violate the proportions of a door. When the whole thing is finished, people trained in formalist attitudes will look at it and say, OK, that works, or it rings true spatially, etc. For me, it rings true spatially, etc., because it's true on twelve other levels at the same time. I find it difficult to unravel the strings. . . .

They are portraits; yet, I don't do details by which we ordinarily recognize people. They're portraits in the same way that you recognize a friend walking down the street from a block away. It would be relatively simple using this method to make uncannily accurate portrait sculpture. Mostly portrait sculpture is aimed at putting the sitter's best foot forward and most sitters who are paying hard cash for a portrait are not interested in psychological probing. I suppose that's the reason I avoid straight sculpture as much as I can, unless the person posing for me is willing to accept my particular kind of treatment (which is generally kind, but not glorifying.)

Phyllis Tuchman, "Interview with George Segal," 1972, pp. 76, 77.

I feel detached from the phrase Pop art and yet I have a fondness for it. It's been ten years since the Pop art movement; it's pronounced dead every season. I look back at it with more warmth and regard than when I lived through it. In retrospect, it was a time of wide-open invention—a new life style—rock music, costuming; a burst of optimism, joyousness. A lot of that innocent frivolity got displaced by violence and cynicism and soberness and political action, assassination, disillusionment. Now we have this law-and-order reaction. What seemed to be heedless, mindless and frivolous in the early '60s will, I think, in retrospect appear as some of the best work ever produced in America. Pop art is a great label for a serious movement that produced a lot of excellent work. Writers responded to the strength, vitality and shock of the new work; they didn't quite understand it. You turn on your TV set to be amused or shocked or entertained. Pop art did a lot of that with its color, its size, its outrageousness. I never believed the magazine definitions of Pop art. When eight, ten or twelve talents emerge, they're called a school. But each one is incredibly different the way Rothko is different from de Kooning. What's called Pop art is a clustering of very different individuals. And, after the public excitement dies down, each man is always thrust on his own resources.

Phyllis Tuchman, "POP! Interviews with George Segal, Andy Warhol, Roy Lichtenstein, James Rosenquist, and Robert Indiana," 1974, p. 25.

I love the plaster because it's a completely characterless material that can pick up any texture that is given to it, so that the sides are cast against the grainy ply-wood and they reek of wood. The backgrounds feel like rough stone-wall and the flesh feels like flesh. And it's all one material which is infinite. Well, it's a pleasure to stumble on a material that in sculpture can refer to every kind of texture, every kind of experience, in the same way that oil-paint is infinite in its possibility: it can either be paint or it can be illusion of any surface. Well, that's delight in the basic material involved with that.

Christian Geelhaar, "Marriage between Matter and Spirit: Interview with George Segal," 1976, p. 234.

The aura I got from the Abstract Expressionist painters was the hope that American painting could challenge and possibly surpass the school of Paris. And these New York upstarts were insisting that here was a new impulse that could touch spontaneity, it could be rhythm, movements, it could be abstract, it could be very large canvases. It could be radical, but by some kind of magic and connection with surrealist ideas, by some kind of connection with difficult, profound ideas that were learned from Europe, Americans for the first time in history could stop being provincial and could deal in religious illumination. They could be anti-materialist, they could be soaring, they could put their finger on the rhythm of the universe, and it was an achievement and accomplishment that had nothing to do with making a lot of money, becoming comfortable or surrounding yourself with cars and objects. But it had to do with an exalted state of mind. That was the ambition, I think, or that's the way I received the message. I was instantly enormously attracted to that.

Malcolm N. Carter, "Creators on Creating: George Segal," 1981, p. 28.

The reason I admire [Hopper] so much is that he never stopped looking at the real world—with all the danger of being a naturalistic illustrator. Now, there's a difference being an illustrator (and he made his living that way and it must have caused him untold private agony). But, for him to use the real stuff of the world and somehow—not suddenly but painstakingly, painfully, slowly—figure out how to stack the elements into a heap that began talking very tellingly of his own deepest inner feelings, he had to make some kind of marriage between what he could see outside with his eyes, touch with his hands, and the feelings that were going on inside. Now, I think that's as simply as I can say what I think art is about.

Gail Levin, ed., "Artists' Panel," 1981, p. 151.

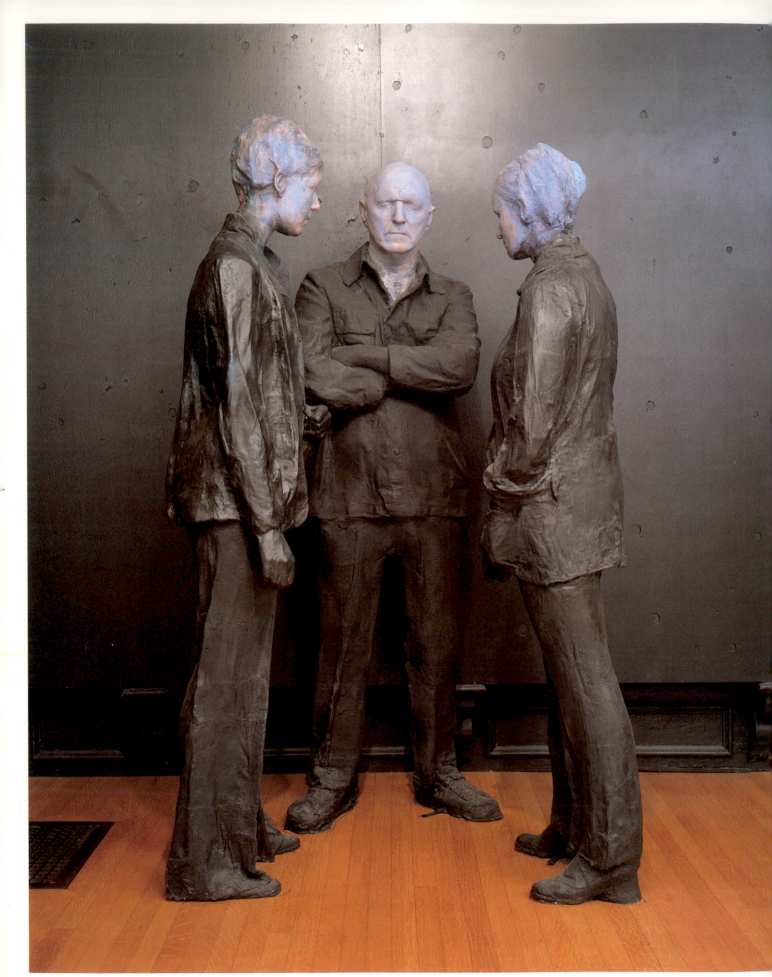

Notes on Technique

George Segal's sculptures often take months to complete. Although he begins a work with a rough idea of what he is seeking, many variables affect the final disposition of a piece. Each stage of the lengthy process is informed by what preceded it. Segal has said, "... the figure is only one of the things that punctuates the space. I work for a long time and eventually there is nothing I can subtract; whatever is left there has to be there."[1]

Once he has a situation in mind, Segal carefully selects someone to pose because "A person's inner set of attitudes comes out in the plaster somehow. ... I am dependent on the sensitivity and response of the person posing for me."[2] When a friend, relative, or model—an art student or someone else referred to him—comes to his studio, Segal describes the situation he envisions. About *Street Meeting* (1977), for which she posed, fine-arts advisor Nancy Rosen has recalled that one of the three figures had been cast before she arrived, but its surface had not yet been painted nor had the backdrop been fabricated. "When George was posing me," she recently recounted, "he said I should stand in relation to this man." He also told her that their heads would eventually be "floating like three apples in this environment."[3]

A figure is generally cast in three stages; each takes about forty-five minutes. Once a pose is determined, the feet are traced on the concrete floor, because the upper torso is usually done first. The lower torso is next, and finally, the head. Exposed flesh and hair are covered with Nivea cream so that the plaster can be removed painlessly. When he served as his first model in 1961, the artist later mentioned, "I knew nothing about the fact that plaster sticks to hair, and I am hairy from head to foot, so it [was] like pulling off a giant bandaid."[4] Since clothing sometimes remains encased within the plaster, someone posing is generally asked to wear old clothes they are willing to leave behind. (When her portrait was taken in 1965, Ethel Scull lost a pair of prized Courrèges boots.)

Segal coats his models with Johnson and Johnson medical bandages that have been treated with plaster and need only to be dipped into pails of warm water before being shaped on a body. He likes the way that plaster flows like water and dries like a rock. How many and which details are captured depends on his touch—how

109. *Street Meeting*, 1977
Painted plaster and painted wood, 96 x 95 x 52 in.
Bruce and Judith Eissner

hard or gently he presses down. To remove each section, seams are cut. When they are later reattached, gesture can be modified because the wafer-thin molds are malleable. Nevertheless, once dried and joined, the casts are durable, although they must stay indoors where conditions can be controlled.

A figure can be cast quickly, but the pliable molds frequently take weeks to reassemble. Segal has said, ". . . I have to fasten everything together and reconstruct the gesture. The angle at which a head is set on a neck can be crucial about the mental life of that person. Each figure becomes a complete reinvention of my ideas of that person." Once the forms are cast, objects and other environmental elements are either chosen or constructed to interact with them. All must work well together, and all must fulfill the formal needs of a work of art.

Throughout the 1960s Segal used the original plaster casts for his figures, which meant that the most detailed features remained in the interiors. Thus, in 1973, the artist could say, "I don't do the details by which we ordinarily recognize people. They're portraits in the same way that you recognize a friend walking down the street from a block away."[5] Soon afterward, however, Segal modified his procedure. Now, after the original cast has been made, the outside is usually built up to make the mold stronger, and then hydrostone, an industrial plaster, is poured into the inside, which is like a three-dimensional photo negative. The skin pores and wrinkles that were in the interior of the original now appear on the new exterior. When the hydrostone has dried, the bandages are peeled off and thrown away. As Segal explained in 1975, "In my earlier work, especially the environmental pieces, I was after a sense of place and the shape of empty air. . . . The portraiture was in the gesture of the figures, which was massive, with sloping shoulders and backs. With the new things, I'm getting more interested in getting subtle nuance. When I work from the inside of the casts, I get much more involved with sensitivity—crevices and rhythms—which can add up to very effective portraiture."[6]

When asked what it was like to be cast, art dealer Richard Bellamy—who has posed for a portrait, *The Costume Party*, *The Sun Bathers*, and *The Holocaust*—responded, "It didn't hurt. Putting yourself in George's hands is one of the safest things you can do. He's no dentist." According to Bellamy, "you could fall asleep if you were tired. It's very peaceful. There's little talking." "Photographs engage your vanity," he adds. "George's castings don't engage your vanity."

Nancy Rosen's remarks echo Bellamy's. "George comforts you," she says. "He is not a ruthless technician. One reason he probably doesn't use strangers is his need for rapport." Rosen never saw her cast self assembled and unpainted. When she finally encountered *Street Meeting*, the bodies were painted black and the heads, a bluish-pink tint. Did she recognize her doppelganger? No, because it is "not verisimilitude that Segal is after." Rather, she points out, "It's some aspect of you that George gets. Also, I was one element interacting with other elements and this was not a real incident in my life."

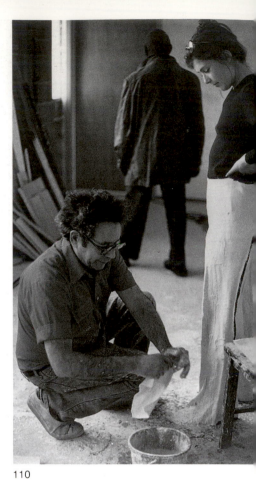

110

111

110–13. Views of *Street Meeting* being cast.
Photographs courtesy of Blackwood Productions

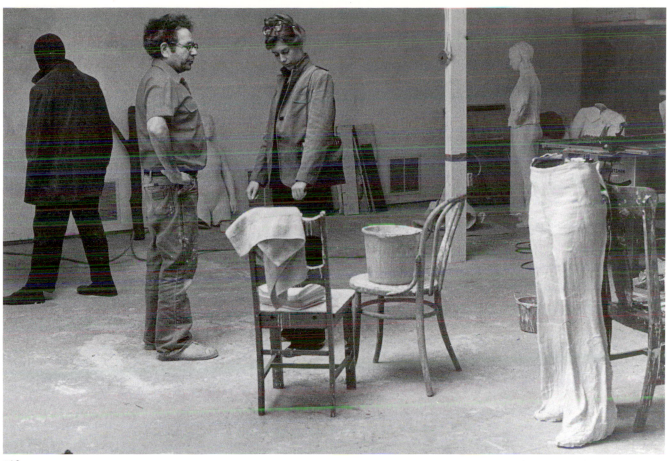

112

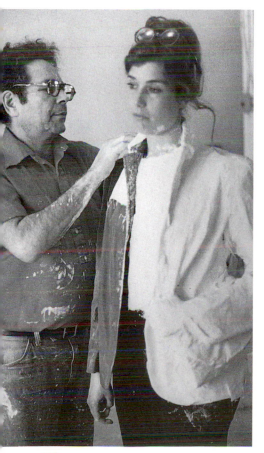

113

To the question, "Did you ever think of casting the ideal man or the ideal woman?" Segal once replied, "... when I started casting people, I discovered that ordinary human beings with no great pretensions of being handsome were somehow singing and beautiful in their rhythms. The people that I prefer to use again and again as models are friends [and relatives] with a very lively mental life. . . . I discovered that I had to totally respect the entity of a specific human being, and it's a whole other set of insights, a whole other set of attitudes. It's a different idea of beauty and it has to do with the gift of life, the gift of consciousness, the gift of a mental life."[7]

NOTES

1. Barbaralee Diamonstein, "George Segal," p. 359.

2. Segal, "Perspectives," pp. 148–49.

3. Unless otherwise indicated, this and all subsequent quotes come from conversations the author has had with the artist and others during the past two years.

4. Diamonstein, "Segal," p. 361.

5. Tuchman, "Interview," p. 77.

6. Gerrit Henry, ed., "The Artist and the Face," p. 36.

7. Diamonstein, "Segal," p. 366.

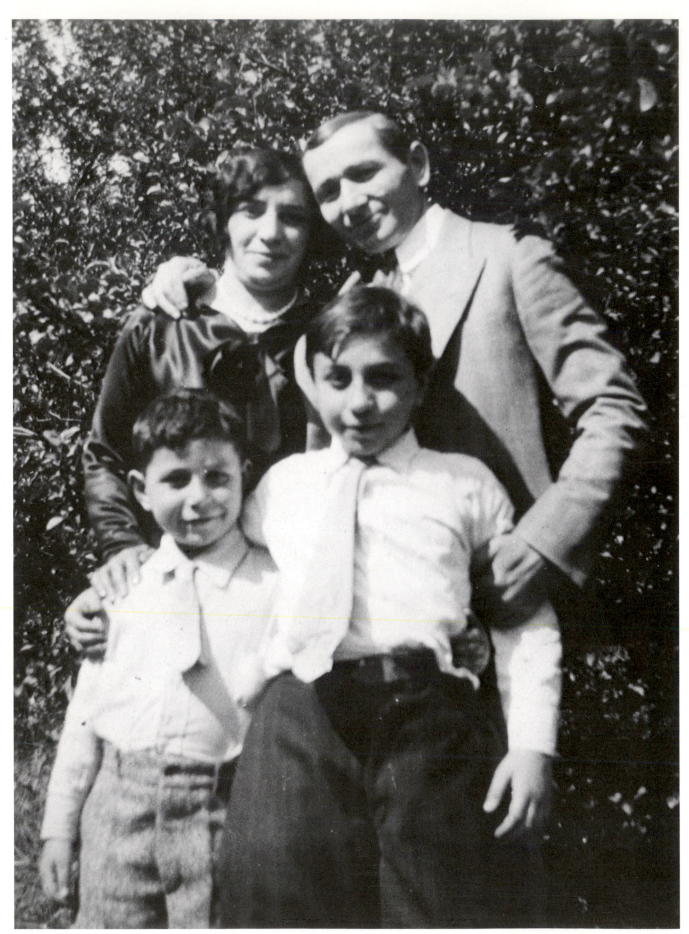

Chronology By Anna Brooke

1924 November 26—born in New York to Jacob and Sophie Gerstenfeld Segal. His father is of Russian Polish extraction and owns a kosher butcher shop in the Bronx. Has one older brother, Morris.

1930–40 Grows up on 174th Street, east of the Concourse. Family moves several times, but always in the same neighborhood. Attends P.S. 70 in the Bronx and Stuyvesant High School in Manhattan, a public school with competitive entrance exams. Majors in art.

1940 Moves with family to South Brunswick, New Jersey, where his father starts a chicken farm. Meets Helen Steinberg, the daughter of a neighboring farmer.

1941 Finishes high school in Brooklyn while living with his aunt. Makes a small plaster figure, which he still owns.

1941–42 Studies at Cooper Union in Manhattan. Leaves school to work on the chicken farm when his brother is drafted into the army.

1944 Graduates from Cooper Union.

1942–46 Studies part-time at Rutgers University, New Brunswick, New Jersey. Interested in philosophy, history, literature.

1946 April 7—marries Helen Steinberg.

1947–48 Studies art education at Pratt Institute of Design, Brooklyn.

1948–49 Studies at New York University School of Education and graduates with a B.S. degree in art education. Fellow students include Larry Rivers and Alfred Leslie; Tony Smith and William Baziotes are among their instructors. Attends sessions of The Club, near campus.

1949 Buys a chicken farm across the road from his father, and devotes all his time to making it successful. Spends six months building facilities, which are now his studio.

1950 Son, Jeffrey, is born.

1953 Meets Allan Kaprow, who is teaching at Rutgers University and living nearby. Kaprow, a founder of the Hansa Gallery, a New York artists' cooperative, introduces him to other members. Forms friendship with Jan Muller. Begins painting seriously again. Daughter, Rena (now a painter), is born.

1955 Teaches an adult art class at Highland Park Community Center (continues for several years).

1956 February—first solo exhibition held at Hansa Gallery. June—included in first group exhibition, at Boston Arts Festival. Summer—goes to Provincetown, Massachusetts (returns every summer through 1959); visits Hans Hofmann's studio there. Starts long association at Rutgers as advisor for drawing and painting at the Fine Arts Club.

1957 March—included in *The New York School: Second Generation*, an important group exhibition organized by Meyer Schapiro for the Jewish Museum, New York.

1957–58 To avoid bankruptcy, teaches English at Jamesburg High School.

1958 Summer—sells his chickens. Converts coops into a painting studio and also makes sculpture with plaster, burlap, and chicken wire. Allan Kaprow stages the first "Happening" on Segal's farm during a Hansa Gallery picnic. Teaches industrial arts at Piscataway High School (until 1961).

1959 October—participates in Allan Kaprow's *18 Happenings in 6 Parts*, Reuben Gallery. Hansa Gallery closes. December—included for the first time in the *Annual Exhibition of Contemporary American Painting*, Whitney Museum of American Art, New York.

1960 Robert Frank spends six months at Segal's farm filming *The Sin of Jesus*, for which

Segal builds some sets. November—first solo exhibition held at Green Gallery, New York, a gallery newly opened by Richard Bellamy, a former director of the Hansa.

1961 Summer—teaches adult painting class in New Brunswick. Given medical bandages newly developed by the chemist husband of one of his Highland Park students and discovers their use as art material. July—serves as his own model for his first work from a live model, *Man at a Table*, made from plaster-dipped bandages applied by his wife at Segal's direction.

1961–64 Teaches art at Roosevelt Junior High School.

1962 Receives Walter K. Gutman Foundation grant. Enrolls in M.F.A. program at Rutgers University. October—included in *New Realists*, the first important Pop art exhibition, held at Sidney Janis Gallery, New York.

1963 January—thesis exhibition of paintings, pastels, and sculpture held at Douglass College, Rutgers University, New Brunswick. Receives M.F.A. degree from Rutgers. April—participates in panel discussion on Pop art at Festival of the Arts in Education, Teachers College, Columbia University, New York City. Fall—makes first trip to Europe (Paris, Düsseldorf, and Venice). Meets Alberto Giacometti in Paris. September—included in the *VII Bienal*, São Paulo, Brazil. October—first solo exhibition in Europe held at Galerie Ileana Sonnabend, Paris. French custom officials had detained *Woman in a Restaurant Booth* for over two weeks, demanding duty for furniture.

1964 Teaches at Hunter College. Devotes himself entirely to sculpture. Major articles appear in *Artnews*, *Art International*, and *Artforum*. Moderna Museet, Stockholm, buys *Man on a Bicycle*, his first museum purchase.

1965 Commissioned to create a double portrait of Robert and Ethel Scull, which receives much publicity when completed. October 8–11

—participates in New York University seminar on elementary and secondary school education in the visual arts. After the Green Gallery closes, begins to exhibit regularly with Sidney Janis Gallery. Wins Neysa McNein Purchase Award from the Whitney Museum for an untitled pastel of 1964. Participates in Sarasota symposium on "environmental sculpture" (continues to participate in various symposia periodically).

1966   Wins first prize of the Frank G. Logan medal and $5000 at the *68th American Exhibition,* Art Institute of Chicago, for *The Truck.* Receives List Art Poster Program Commission.

1967   September—included in the *IX Bienal,* São Paulo. Designs a three-dimensional poster using display lights to announce a series of Happenings by Allan Kaprow for the Institute of Contemporary Art, Boston.

1968   April—first solo museum exhibition, *George Segal: 12 Human Situations,* held at the Museum of Contemporary Art, Chicago. Designs a Lincoln Center poster for the New York City Ballet.

1968–69   Is Lecturer in Creative Arts, Sculpture, at Princeton University. *Cinema* is placed at the entrance to a large Pop art exhibition organized by the Hayward Gallery, London.

1969   Receives List Award.

1970   Receives honorary doctorate from Rutgers University. Visits the large Matisse exhibition at the Grand Palais, Paris.

1971   *Man on a Printing Press* commissioned by the Des Moines Register and Tribune Company.

1971–72   Major solo traveling exhibition, organized by the Kunsthaus, Zurich, tours around Europe; Segal supervises installations in Paris, Munich, Cologne, Rotterdam, Leverkusen, and Tübingen.

1972   Is Distinguished Visiting Professor for one semester, City University of New York.

1973   Invited to Israel by Tel Aviv Foundation for Literature and Art and commissioned to create a work, *Sacrifice of Isaac.* Casts first bronze (later permanently installed in Bruce Park), for an outdoor sculpture show in Greenwich, Connecticut.

1974   Fall—first tapestry, *Girl with Red Towel,* woven by Atelier de St. Cyr, is produced by Tapestry Associates, New York, in an edition of six. Designs a plastic relief poster for the Saint Louis Symphony.

1976   June—dedication held for *The Restaurant* at Federal Building Plaza, Buffalo, New York, a GSA commission. November—visits Soviet Union as an American Specialist under the State Department's Eastern European Programs Cultural Exchange Program.

1977   Selected with Leonard Baskin, Robert Graham, and Neil Estern to make sculpture for the FDR Memorial in Washington, D.C. First solo museum exhibition of pastels organized and circulated by the Art Galleries, California State University, Long Beach.

1978   October—major solo exhibition held at the Walker Art Center, Minneapolis, with tour to San Francisco Museum of Modern Art and Whitney Museum of American Art; Segal supervises installations. Kent State University Board rejects sculpture *In Memory of May 4, 1970, Kent State: Abraham and Isaac,* a memorial to four demonstrators killed at Kent State University in 1970 by National Guardsmen; Princeton University accepts it. Makes eleven prints from live models at 2RC editions, Rome.

1979   Newark Museum commissions *Toll Booth. Hand on Buttocks,* a cast-paper multiple made at 2RC in Rome, is published by Metropolitan Museum of Art. July—commissioned by Mildred Andrews Fund to create homosexual liberation monument for Sheridan Square, New York City. October 5—dedication held for *Abraham and Isaac* at Princeton University.

1980   May 14—dedication held for *The Steelmakers,* Youngstown, Ohio, Federal Plaza Mall; Segal is given key to the city. *Appalachian Farm Couple—1936,* originally exe-cuted as part of the FDR Memorial, is bought by the Neuberger Museum in Purchase, New York, after 4,300 visitors to the gallery vote for its acquisition from a group of forty-three other works of art.

1981   Travels to China as part of a United States government exchange program. Elected to the American Institute of Arts and Letters, New York, and to the American Academy of Arts and Sciences, Cambridge, Massachusetts. Travels to Japan.

1982   Receives Skowhegan Medal for Sculpture. April—*Next Departure* is installed in the Port Authority Terminal Building, New York. Supervises the installations of a retrospective circulated throughout Japan.

1983   January—his tableau with computers is on the cover of *Time* magazine's *Man of the Year* issue. *The Holocaust* is installed in Golden Gate Park, San Francisco.

1985   *The Constructors* is installed in the new Department of Commerce Building, Trenton, New Jersey.

1989   Receives the New Jersey Governor's Walt Whitman Creative Arts Award.

1991   Receives Distinguished Alumnus Award from New York University and the Order of Andres Bello, First Class, from the Republic of Venezuela.

1992   Receives honorary doctorate from State University of New York at Purchase and International Lifetime Achievement Award for Sculpture from the International Sculpture Center, Washington, D.C.

1994   Receives honorary doctorate from Massachusetts College of Fine Arts, Boston.

1997   Receives Praemium Imperiale Award for lifetime achievement in the arts, Tokyo. *Depression Bread Line, Appalachian Farm Couple—1936,* and *Fireside Chat* are installed as part of the FDR Memorial in Washington, D.C. Major traveling solo exhibition opens at the Montreal Museum of Fine Arts.

114.   Segal with his mother, father, and older brother, 1930s (p. 116)

Exhibitions

Smithsonian Institution, Washington, D.C.; Jewish Museum, New York; Miami Art Museum.

Selected Group Exhibitions

1956

New England Exhibition of Painting, Sculpture, Drawing, and Graphic Arts, Boston Arts Festival, June 9–24.

1957

The New York School: Second Generation, Jewish Museum, New York, March 10–April 28.

1959

1959 Annual Exhibition of Contemporary American Painting, Whitney Museum of American Art, New York, December 9–January 31, 1960.

Below Zero, Reuben Gallery, New York, December 18–January 5, 1960.

1960

Paintings, Reuben Gallery, New York, January 29–February 18.

1961

Work by New Jersey Artists 1961: 4th Triennial State-Wide Juried Exhibition, Newark Museum, May 5–June 11.

1962

Figures, Kornblee Gallery, New York, May–June.

The New Realists, Sidney Janis Gallery, New York, October 31–December 1.

1963

66th Annual American Exhibition, Art Institute of Chicago, January 11–February 10. Also included in 1966, 1974, 1976.

New Works II, Green Gallery, New York, January 29–February 16.

VII Bienal de São Paulo, Museu de Arte Moderna, São Paulo, Brazil, September–December. Also included in 1967.

1964

Four Environments by Four New Realists, Sidney Janis Gallery, New York, January 6–31.

Amerikansk pop-konst, Moderna Museet, Stockholm, February 29–April 12, and tour.

The Ten U.S.A. Sculptors of the 1963 São Paulo Bienal, Howard Wise Gallery, New York, March 5–28.

New Work: Part III, Green Gallery, New York, April 8–May 2.

Recent American Drawings, Rose Art Museum, Brandeis University, Waltham, Massachusetts, April 19–May 17.

Recent American Sculpture, Jewish Museum, New York, October 15–November 29.

1964 Pittsburgh International Exhibition of Contemporary Painting and Sculpture, Museum of Art, Carnegie Institute, Pittsburgh, October 30–January 10, 1965. Also included in 1967, 1970.

Three Generations: A Selection of 20th Century Art, Sidney Janis Gallery, New York, November 24–December 26.

1964 Annual Exhibition of Contemporary American Sculpture, Whitney Museum of American Art, New York, December 9–January 31, 1965. Also included in 1966, 1968, 1970.

1965

Eleven from the Reuben Gallery, Solomon R. Guggenheim Museum, New York, January.

New American Realism, Worcester Art Museum, Worcester, Massachusetts, February 18–April 4.

Pop Art and the American Tradition, Milwaukee Art Center, April 9–May 9.

A Decade of American Drawings, 1955–1965, Whitney Museum of American Art, New York, April 28–June 6.

Etats-Unis Sculptures du XXe siècle, Musée Rodin, Paris, June 22–October 10, and Museum of Modern Art International Council tour.

Selected Works by Contemporary New Jersey Artists 1965, Newark Museum, November 18–January 2, 1966.

Pop and Op, Sidney Janis Gallery, New York, December.

1966

Recent Still Life, Museum of Art, Rhode Island School of Design, Providence, February 23–April 4.

Erotic Art, Sidney Janis Gallery, New York, October 3–29.

Eight Sculptors: The Ambiguous Image, Walker Art Center, Minneapolis, October 22–December 4.

1967

Dine Segal Oldenburg: Painting/Sculpture, Art Gallery of Ontario, Toronto, January 14–February 12, and tour.

American Sculpture of the Sixties, Los Angeles County Museum of Art, April 28–June 25, and tour.

7 for 67: Works by Contemporary Sculptors, City Art Museum, Saint Louis, October 1–November 12.

Guggenheim International Exhibition 1967: Sculpture from 20 Nations, Solomon R. Guggenheim Museum, New York, October 20–February 4, 1968, and tour.

Protest and Hope, New School for Social Research, New York, October 24–December 2.

List Art Posters, New School for Social Research, New York, November 20–December 8.

Homage to Marilyn Monroe, Sidney Janis Gallery, New York, December 6–30.

1968

Documenta 4, Museum Fridericianum, Kassel, West Germany, June 27–October 6.

1969

XXth Century Art from the Nelson A. Rockefeller Collection, Museum of Modern Art, New York, May 28–September 1.

Pop Art, Hayward Gallery, London, July 9–September 3, and Arts Council tour.

La Nouvelle Figuration américaine: Peinture, sculpture, film, 1963–1968, Palais des Beaux-Arts, Brussels, October–November.

New York Painting and Sculpture: 1940–1970, Metropolitan Museum of Art, New York, October 18–February 1, 1970.

1970

Figures Environments, Walker Art Center, Minneapolis, May 15–June 13, and tour.

Pop art, nouveau réalisme, nieuwe figuratie, Palais des Beaux-Arts, Brussels, June–September.

1971

Métamorphose de l'objet: Art et anti-art, 1910–1970, Palais des Beaux-Arts, Brussels, April 22–June 6, and tour.

IVe Exposition internationale de sculpture contemporaine, Musée Rodin, Paris, July 7–September 30.

Paintings by Richard Anuszkiewicz, Sculpture by George Segal, New Jersey State Museum, Trenton, September 18–November 19.

White on White: The White Monochrome in the 20th Century, Museum of Contemporary Art, Chicago, December 18–January 30, 1972.

1972

Abstract Expressionism and Pop Art, Sidney Janis Gallery, New York, February 9–March 4.

Green Gallery Revisited, Emily Lowe Gallery, Hofstra University, Hempstead, Long Island, New York, February 22–March 29.

1973

American Art Third Quarter-Century, Seattle Art Museum, August 22–October 14.

New York Collection for Stockholm, Moderna Museet, Stockholm, October 27–December 2.

Contemporary American Artists, Cleveland Museum of Art, December 18–February 10, 1974.

1974

Ars 74, Ateneum, Suomen Taideakatemia, Helsinki, February 15–March 31, and tour.

1975

Three Centuries of the American Nude, Minneapolis Institute of the Arts, May 9–July 13, and tour.

Traditions and Revisions: Themes from the History of Sculpture, Cleveland Museum of Art, September 23–November 16.

Sculpture: American Directions, 1945–1975, National Collection of Fine Arts, Smithsonian Institution, Washington, D.C., October 8–November 30.

25 Stills, Whitney Museum Downtown, New York, October 30–December 3.

1976

200 Years of American Sculpture, Whitney Museum of Art, New York, March 16–September 26.

Materials and Techniques of 20th-Century Artists, Cleveland Museum of Art, November 17–February 2, 1977.

1977

The Chosen Object: European and American Still-Life, Joslyn Art Museum, Omaha, April 23–June 5.

1978

Art about Art, Whitney Museum of American Art, New York, July 19–September 24, and tour.

1979

Sensuous Sculpture: Mary Frank, Larry Rivers, George Segal, Alex Rosenberg Gallery, New York, February 7–March 3.

Contemporary Sculpture: Selections from the Collection of the Museum of Modern Art, Museum of Modern Art, New York, May 18–August 7.

1980

Seven Decades of Twentieth-Century Art from the Sidney and Harriet Janis Collection of the Museum of Modern Art and the Sidney Janis Gallery Collection, La Jolla Museum of Contemporary Art, La Jolla, California, March 28–May, and tour.

Sculpture on the Wall: Relief Sculpture of the Seventies, University Galleries, University of Massachusetts at Amherst, March 29–May 4.

Pop Art: Evoluzione de una generazione, Palazzo Grassi, Venice, Summer.

1981

Real, Really Real and Super Real, San Antonio Museum of Art, San Antonio, Texas, March 1–April 26.

Exhibition of Work by Newly Elected Members and Recipients of Honors and Awards, American Academy and Institute of Arts and Letters, New York, May 20–June 14.

Contemporary American Realism since 1960, Pennsylvania Academy of the Fine Arts, Philadelphia, September 18–December 13.

1982

Sculpture: New Acquisitions, Metropolitan Museum of Art, New York, April 6–Spring 1983.

Five Artists and the Figure: Duane Hanson, Alex Katz, Philip Pearlstein, Alice Neel, George Segal, Whitney Museum of American Art, Fairfield County, Stamford, Connecticut, April 9–June 9.

Prints by Contemporary Sculptors, Yale University Art Gallery, New Haven, Connecticut,

May 18–August 31.

Casting: A Survey of Cast Metal Sculpture in the 80's, Fuller Goldeen Gallery, San Francisco, July 8–August 28.

1984

Six in Bronze, Williams College Museum of Art, Williamstown, Massachusetts, January 15–February 26, and tour.

Figurative Sculpture: Ten Artists/Two Decades, University Art Museum, California State University, Long Beach, March 12–April 29.

1985

Body and Soul: Aspects of Recent Figurative Sculpture, Contemporary Arts Center, Cincinnati, September 6–October 12, and tour.

Contemporary Bronze: Six in the Figurative Tradition, Sheldon Memorial Art Gallery, University of Nebraska, Lincoln, November 19–January 19, 1986, and tour.

1988

Italian Pavilion, Venice Biennale, June 26–September 25.

1991

The Pop Art Show, Royal Academy of Arts, London, September 13–December 15, and tour.

Public Collections

Aachen, Germany, Neue Galerie-Sammlung Ludwig
Aachen, Germany, Suermondt-Ludwig-Museum
Akron, Ohio, Akron Art Institute
Amsterdam, The Netherlands, Stedelijk Museum
Bloomington, Indiana, Indiana University Art Museum
Buffalo, New York, Albright-Knox Art Gallery
Buffalo, New York, Federal Office Building
Chicago, Illinois, Art Institute of Chicago
Chicago, Illinois, Museum of Contemporary Art
Cleveland, Ohio, Cleveland Museum of Art
Cleveland, Ohio, Justice Center
Cologne, Germany, Kölnisches Stadtmuseum
Cologne, Germany, Wallraf Richartz Museum
Darmstadt, Germany, Hessisches Landesmuseum

Des Moines, Iowa, Des Moines Art Center
Des Moines, Iowa, Des Moines Register and Tribune
Detroit, Michigan, Detroit Institute of Arts
Greenwich, Connecticut, City of Greenwich
Hanover, New Hampshire, Dartmouth College Museum and Galleries
Hartford, Connecticut, Wadsworth Atheneum
Helsinki, Finland, Ateneumin Taidemuseo
Krefeld, Germany, Kaiser Wilhelm Museum
Long Beach, California, Art Museum and Galleries, California State University
Mexico City, Mexico, Tamayo Museum
Milwaukee, Wisconsin, Milwaukee Art Center
Minneapolis, Minnesota, Walker Art Center
Mönchengladbach, Germany, Städtisches Museum Mönchengladbach
Munich, Germany, Staatsgalerie Moderner Kunst
New York City, New York, Jewish Museum

New York City, New York, Metropolitan Museum of Art
New York City, New York, Museum of Modern Art
New York City, New York, Port Authority Bus Terminal
New York City, New York, Solomon R. Guggenheim Museum
New York City, New York, Whitney Museum of American Art
Newark, New Jersey, Newark Museum
Omaha, Nebraska, Joslyn Art Museum
Osaka, Japan, National Museum of Art
Ottawa, Canada, National Gallery of Canada
Paris, France, Centre Georges Pompidou, Musée National d'Art Moderne
Pasadena, California, Norton Simon Museum of Art
Philadelphia, Pennsylvania, Philadelphia Museum of Art
Pittsburgh, Pennsylvania, Carnegie Institute
Princeton, New Jersey, Art Museum, Princeton University
Purchase, New York, Neuberger Museum
Rotterdam, The Netherlands, Museum Boymans-van Beuningen
San Francisco, California, San Francisco Museum of Modern Art
Stockholm, Sweden, Moderna Museet
Stuttgart, Germany, Staatsgalerie Stuttgart
Tel Aviv, Israel, Mann Auditorium
Tokyo, Japan, Hara Museum of Contemporary Art
Tokyo, Japan, Seibu Museum of Art
Toronto, Canada, Art Gallery of Ontario
Trenton, New Jersey, New Jersey State Museum
Vancouver, Canada, Vancouver Art Gallery
Washington, D.C., Hirshhorn Museum and Sculpture Garden, Smithsonian Institution
Washington, D.C., Library of Congress
Washington, D.C., National Gallery of Art
Washington, D.C., National Museum of American Art, Smithsonian Institution
Wuppertal, Germany, Von der Heydt-Museum der Stadt Wuppertal
Yonkers, New York, Hudson River Museum
Youngstown, Ohio, City of Youngstown
Zurich, Switzerland, Kunsthaus

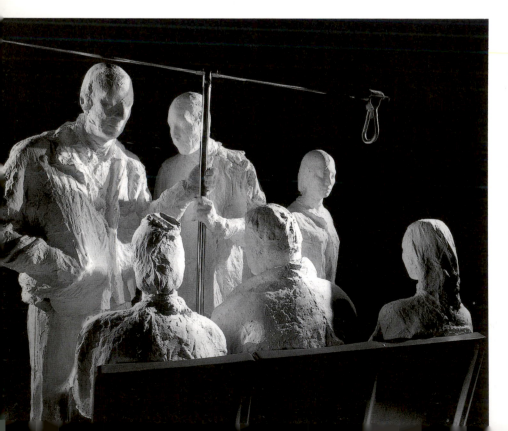

115. *Bus Passengers* (detail), 1997
Plaster, metal, and plastic, 80½ x 68 x 52 in.
Courtesy Sidney Janis Gallery, New York

Selected Bibliography

Interviews and Statements

Baigell, Matthew. "Segal's Holocaust Memorial." *Art in America* 71 (summer 1983): 134–36. Interview.

Baker, Elizabeth C. "Larry Rivers and George Segal: Back in the U.S.S.R." *Art in America* 65 (November–December 1977): 104–12. Interview.

Bellamy, Richard. "Excerpt from a Conversation . . . *Girl on a Chair*," brochure. New York and London: Editions Alecto Limited, 1970.

Berger, Danny. "George Segal: An Interview." *Print Collector's Newsletter* 18 (July–August 1987): 91–94.

Carter, Malcolm N. "Creators on Creating: George Segal." *Saturday Review* 8 (May 1981): 26–30.

Catoir, Barbara. "Interview mit George Segal." *Das Kunstwerk* 24 (May 1971): 3–8.

Coplans, John. "George Segal: An Interview." *Dialogue: Ohio's Art Journal* (March–April 1980): 4–6. On the occasion of an exhibition at the Akron Art Institute.

Crossman, Christopher B., and Nancy E. Miller. "A Conversation with George Segal." *Albright-Knox Art Gallery, Gallery Studies* 1 (October 1977): 11–17.

Diamonstein, Barbaralee. "George Segal." *Inside New York's Art World*. New York: Rizzoli, 1979, pp. 354–66. Interview.

Dypréau, Jean. "Métamorphoses: L'Ecole de New York, un film de Jean Antoine." *Quadrum* 18 (1965): 161–64. Statement.

Geelhaar, Christian. "Marriage between Matter and Spirit: Interview with George Segal." *Pantheon* 34 (July 1976): 231–37.

Geldzahler, Henry. "An Interview with George Segal." *Artforum* 3 (November 1964): 26–29. Reprinted in *Quadrum* 19 (1965): 115–16.

Glenn, C. W. "Artist's Dialogue: A Conversation with George Segal." *Architectural Digest* 40 (November 1983): 66, 70, 74, 76.

Glueck, Grace, ed. "The 20th-Century Artists Most Admired by Other Artists." *Artnews* 76 (November 1977): 101. Statement.

———. "The Artist's Artists." *Artnews* 81 (November 1982): 100. Statement.

Henry, Gerrit, ed. "The Artist and the Face: A Modern Sampling." *Art in America* 63 (January–February 1975): 34–36. Interview.

———. "Is New York Still the Artistic Place to Be?: Twelve Artists in and around the Metropolitan Area Discuss How the City Inspires Their Work and What Defines New York as an Esthetic Environment." *Artnews* 75 (November 1976): 42–47. Statement.

———. "Paper in Transition." *Print Collector's Newsletter* 10 (July–August 1979): 83–86. Statement.

Levin, Gail, ed. "Artists' Panel: Joel Meyerowitz, Photographer; George Segal, Sculptor; William Bailey, Painter; Moderator, Gail Levin." *Art Journal* 41 (summer 1981): 150–54. Symposium held October 27, 1980, at the Whitney Museum of American Art.

Rose, Barbara. "Psychological Sculpture: The Artist Whose Plaster People Have Pop-ped Our Self-Images Tells Why, How He Works—in an Inner World." *Vogue* 166 (September 1976): 348–49, 383–88.

———, and Irving Sandler, eds. "Sensibility of the Sixties." *Art in America* 55 (January–February 1967): 44–57. Statement by Segal: "Everyone Shares a Huge Stew of Ideas," p. 55.

Segal, George. Statement in Michel Courtois and Allan Kaprow. *Segal*. Paris: Galerie Ileana Sonnabend, 1963.

———. Statement in "Jackson Pollock: An Artists' Symposium, Part 2." *Artnews* 66 (May 1967): 29, 69–70.

———. "Perspectives on American Sculpture 2. The Sense of 'Why Not?': George Segal on His Art." *Studio International* 174 (October 1967): 146–49. Introduction by William Lipke.

———. Statement on *The Bowery* in *Art Now: New York* 2, no. 6 (1970): 3–4.

———. "Interview: George Segal." In *George Segal*. Cologne: Onnasch Galerie, 1971.

———. "Commentaries on Six Sculptures." In *George Segal: Sculptures*. Minneapolis: Walker Art Center, 1978, pp. 31–55.

———, et al. "The One and the Many: Art and Mass Reproduction." *Artnews* 81 (November 1982): 117–18.

———. "A Sense of Stillness." *Artnews* 82 (summer 1983): 11–12.

———. "On Rembrandt." *Art and Antiques*, September 1987, pp. 80–83.

Tuchman, Phyllis. "Interview with George Segal." *Art in America* 60 (May–June 1972): 74–81.

———. "POP! Interviews with George Segal, Andy Warhol, Roy Lichtenstein, James Rosenquist, and Robert Indiana." *Artnews* 73 (May 1974): 24–29.

Monographs and Solo-Exhibition Catalogs

Barrio-Garay, José Luis, and Delehanty, Suzanne. *George Segal: Environments.* Philadelphia: Institute of Contemporary Art, 1976.

———, and Taylor, John Lloyd. *The Private*

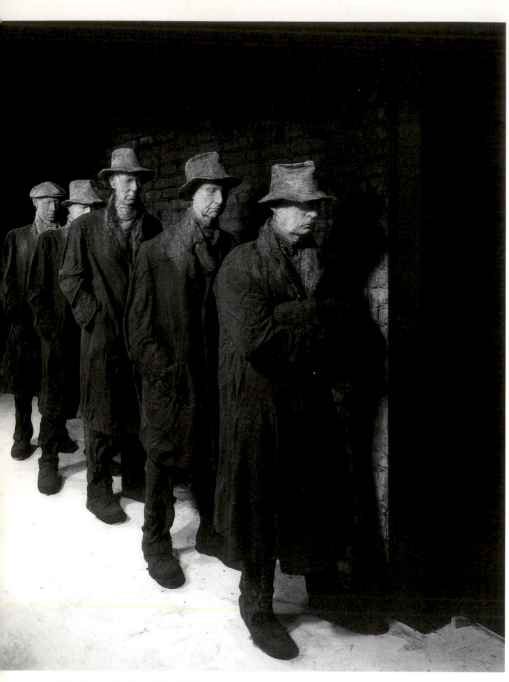

116. *Depression Bread Line,* 1991
Plaster, wood, metal, and acrylic paint,
108 x 148 x 36 in.
Courtesy Sidney Janis Gallery, New York

World of George Segal. Milwaukee: University of Wisconsin, 1973.

Berman, Nancy M. *George Segal: Works from the Bible.* Los Angeles: Skirball Cultural Center, 1997.

Courtois, Michel, Allan Kaprow, George Segal. *Segal.* Paris: Galerie Ileana Sonnabend, 1963.

Exhibition George Segal. New York: Sidney Janis Gallery, 1970.

An Exhibition of New Painted Sculpture by George Segal. New York: Sidney Janis Gallery, 1982.

Exhibition of Recent Sculpture by George Segal. New York: Sidney Janis Gallery, 1977.

Friedman, Martin. *George Segal.* Paris: Galerie Darthea Speyer, 1969.

———, Graham W. J. Beal, and George Segal. *George Segal: Sculptures.* Minneapolis: Walker Art Center, 1978.

George Segal. Jerusalem: Israel Museum, 1983.

George Segal. New York: Sidney Janis, 1986. Introduction by Robert Rosenblum.

George Segal: Neue Skulpturen/New Sculpture. Zurich: Galerie André Emmerich, 1975.

Glenn, Constance, and Maudette Bell. *George Segal: Pastels, 1957–1965.* Long Beach: California State University, 1977.

Hunter, Sam, and Don Hawthorne. *George Segal.* New York: Rizzoli, 1984. Revised edition, 1989.

Kelder, Diane. *George Segal/Blue Jean Series.* Staten Island, N.Y.: Staten Island Museum/College of Staten Island, 1978.

Kelder, Diane, and Danny Berger. *George Segal/Blue Jean Series.* Rome: 2RC, 1976. Includes excerpts from an interview with Barbara Rose.

Kinokuni, Ken-ichi, Masataki Ogawa, and Akira Moriguchi. *George Segal.* Tokyo: Seibu Museum of Art, 1982.

Kreytenberg, Gert. *George Segal: Ruth in Her Kitchen.* Stuttgart: Philipp Reclam, 1970.

Livingstone, Marco. *George Segal, A Retrospective: Sculptures, Paintings, Drawings.* Montreal: Montreal Museum of Fine Arts, 1997.

New Sculpture by George Segal. New York: Sidney Janis Gallery, 1965.

New Sculpture by George Segal. New York: Sidney Janis Gallery, 1968–69.

New Sculpture by George Segal. New York: Sidney Janis Gallery, 1971.

New Sculpture by George Segal. New York: Sidney Janis Gallery, 1973.

New Sculpture by George Segal. New York: Sidney Janis Gallery, 1974.

New Sculpture by George Segal. New York: Sidney Janis Gallery, 1978.

Price, Marla. *George Segal: Still Lifes and Related Works.* Fort Worth: Modern Art Museum of Fort Worth, 1990.

Recent Sculpture in Plaster and Bronze by George Segal. New York: Sidney Janis Gallery, 1980.

Robbe-Grillet, Alain. *George Segal: Invasion blanche.* Paris: Editions de la Différence; Galerie Beaubourg, 1990.

Segal at Janis. New York: Sidney Janis Gallery, 1967.

Seitz, William C. *Segal*. Stuttgart: Gerd Hatje and New York: Harry N. Abrams, 1972.

van der Marck, Jan. *George Segal: 12 Human Situations*. Chicago: Museum of Contemporary Art, 1968.

———. *George Segal*. Zurich: Kunsthaus, 1971.

———. *George Segal*. Tubingen, West Germany: Kunsthalle; Munich: Städtische Galerie im Lenbachhaus, 1972. Revised version of the Zurich catalog.

———. *George Segal*. Paris: Centre National d'Art Contemporain, 1972 (CNAC Archives, no. 5). Revised and translated version of the Zurich catalog.

———. *George Segal*. New York: Harry N. Abrams, 1975. Revised edition, 1979.

Periodicals, Books, and Group-Exhibition Catalogs

Adams, Doug. *Transcendence with the Human Body in Art: George Segal, Stephen de Staebler, Jasper Johns, and Christo*. New York: Crossroad, 1991.

Alloway, Lawrence. "George Segal." *Nation*, June 8, 1970, p. 702. Reprinted in *Topics in American Art since 1945*. New York: W. W. Norton, 1975, pp. 182–84.

Amaya, Mario. "George Segal." In *Pop Art . . . and After*. New York: Viking Press, 1966, pp. 97–99.

Andersen, Wayne. *American Sculpture in Process: 1930/1970*. Boston: New York Graphic Society, 1975.

Asbury, Edith Evans. "Sculpture Planned for 'Village' Brings Objection." *New York Times*, August 28, 1980, sec. B, p. 3. Discussion of *Gay Liberation*, proposed for Christopher Park, in Sheridan Square, New York.

Baigel, Matthew. "Segal's Holocaust Memorial." *Art in America* 71 (March 1983): 134–36.

Brenson, Michael. "Why Segal Is Doing Holocaust Memorial." *New York Times*, April 8, 1983, sec. C, p. 16.

Calas, Elena. "George Segal's Earthbound Ghosts." *Coloquio Artes* (Lisbon) 13 (June 1971): 34–37. Reprinted in *Icons and Images of the Sixties*. New York: E. P. Dutton, 1971, pp. 32–40.

Canaday, John. "Plaster People and Plastic Cuties." *New York Times*, April 25, 1971, sec. D, p. 19.

Carter, Malcolm N. "The F.D.R. Memorial: A Monument to Politics, Bureaucracy and the Art of Accommodation." *Artnews* 77 (October 1978): 50–57. Discussion of the collaboration of landscape architect Lawrence Halprin and sculptors George Segal, Leonard Baskin, Robert Graham, and Neil Estern on a park in Washington, D.C.

"The Casting of Ethel Scull." *Time*, April 1, 1966, p. 69.

de Plessix, Francine, ed. "Painters and Poets." *Art in America* 53 (October–November 1965): 32. Segal coupled with Wallace Stevens, "Angel Surrounded by Paysans."

Elsen, Albert. "'Mind Bending' with George Segal." *Artnews* 76 (February 1977): 34–37.

———. "George Segal Retrospective—'A Sort of Hallucinatory Intensity.'" *Washington Star*, July 22, 1979, sec. E, p. 9. Review of exhibition at the Whitney Museum of American Art, New York.

Friedman, Martin. "Mallary, Segal, Agostini: The Exaltation of the Prosaic." *Art International* 7 (November 10, 1963): 70–71.

———. "George Segal." In *Figures/Environments*. Minneapolis: Walker Art Center, 1970, pp. 16–18.

Geist, William E. "Commuters' Sculpture: Waiting Bus Riders Ponder Its Meaning." *New York Times*, April 27, 1982, sec. B, p. 2. *The Commuters* unveiled at Port Authority Bus Terminal.

Geldzahler, Henry. "George Segal." In *Recent American Sculpture*. New York: Jewish Museum, 1964, pp. 24–27. Reprinted in *Quadrum* 19 (1965): 115–16.

———. *New York Painting and Sculpture: 1940–1970*. New York: Metropolitan Museum of Art, 1969.

"'George Segal Has Hands Like a Surgeon.'" *Artnews* 79 (summer 1980): 7. Discussion of *Toll Booth*, acquired by the Newark Museum.

"Ghost Maker." *Time*, May 11, 1970, p. 72.

Glueck, Grace. "Homosexual-Liberation Statue Is Planned for Sheridan Square." *New York Times*, July 21, 1979, p. 10. Concerning the commissioning of Segal's *Gay Liberation*.

Gruen, John. "Art: A Quiet Environment for Frozen Friends." *New York Herald Tribune Magazine*, March 22, 1964, p. 32. Review of exhibition at Green Gallery.

Henning, Edward B. "*Red Light* by George Segal." *Cleveland Museum of Art Bulletin* 63 (May 1976): 146–50.

Hughes, Robert. "Invasion of the Plaster People." *Time*, August 27, 1979, p. 68.

Hunter, Sam. "George Segal's *Blue Girl on Park Bench*. Transforming the Wasteland into the Space of Dreams." *Artnews* 80 (summer 1981): 136–37.

Johnson, Ellen H. "The Sculpture of George Segal." *Art International* 8 (March 20, 1964): 46–49. Reprinted in *Modern Art and the Object*. New York: Harper and Row, 1976, pp. 164–70.

Kaprow, Allan. "Segal's Vital Mummies." *Artnews* 62 (February 1964): 30–33, 65.

Kingsley, April. "The Great Body Snatcher." *Newsweek*, July 9, 1979, pp. 66–67.

Kramer, Hilton. "Plebeian Figures, Banal Anecdotes: The Tableaux of George Segal." *New York Times*, December 15, 1968, sec. 2, p. 33. Reprinted in *The Age of the Avant Garde: An Art Chronicle of 1956–1972*. New York: Farrar, Straus, and Giroux, 1973, pp. 442–45.

———. "Art: Segal Casts New Role for Color." *New York Times*, December 8, 1978, sec. C, p. 16. Review of exhibition at Sidney Janis Gallery, New York.

———. "When George Segal Goes Public." *New York Times*, October 19, 1980, sec. 2, pp. 33, 36.

Kuspit, Donald B. "George Segal: On the Verge of Tragic Vision." *Art in America* 65 (May–June 1977): 84–85.

———. "George Segal." *Artforum* 22 (September 1983): 72–73.

Livingstone, Marco. *Pop Art: A Continuing History*. London: Thames and Hudson, 1990.

"Modern Plaster Master: Artist Makes a Hit with Lifelike Casts." *Life*, June 19, 1964, pp. 103–7.

O'Doherty, Brian. "Art: Avant-Garde Revolt: 'New Realists' Mock U.S. Mass Culture in Exhibition at Sidney Janis Gallery." *New York Times*, October 31, 1962, p. 41.

"One for the Road." *Time*, August 26, 1966, p. 60.

"People Are Talking About . . . George Segal." *Vogue* 143 (March 15, 1964): 98–99.

Perreault, John. "Plaster Caste." *Artnews* 67 (November 1968): 54–55, 75–76.

———. "George Segal: Plastered People." *Village Voice*, October 24, 1974, pp. 42–43.

Pincus-Witten, Robert. "George Segal." In *Dine Oldenburg Segal: Painting/Sculpture.* Toronto: Art Gallery of Ontario; Buffalo: Albright-Knox Art Gallery, 1967, pp. 55–70. Revised and reprinted as "George Segal as Realist." *Artforum* 5 (summer 1967): 84–87.

"Presences in Plaster." *Time,* December 13, 1968, p. 84. Review of exhibition at Sidney Janis Gallery.

Rauh, Emily S. "George Segal." On *7 for 67.* Saint Louis: Saint Louis Art Museum, 1967.

Robbe-Grillet, Alain. "White Invasion." *Journal of Art* 4 (January 1991): 12–13.

Rose, Barbara. "Dada, Then and Now." *Art International* 7 (January 25, 1963): 23–28.

Rosenberg, Harold. "The Art Galleries: The Game of Illusion." *New Yorker,* November 24, 1962, pp. 161–67. Review of *New Realists* exhibition at Sidney Janis Gallery.

————. "The Art of Bad Conscience." *New Yorker,* December 6, 1967, pp. 138–49. Review of *Protest and Hope* exhibition at New School for Social Research.

Rubinfien, Leo. "On George Segal's Reliefs." *Artforum* 15 (May 1977): 44–45.

Rudikoff, Sonia. "New Realists in New York." *Art International* 7 (January 1963): 39–41.

Russell, John. "George Segal Takes World of Plaster to Whitney." *New York Times,* June 1, 1979, sec. C, pp. 1, 17.

"Sculpture (cont'd.)." *New Yorker,* October 27, 1980, pp. 42–45. Includes statements made at a hearing about the *Gay Liberation* sculpture for Christopher Park.

"The Silent People." *Newsweek,* October 25, 1965, pp. 104, 107.

Solomon, Alan R. "The New American Art." *Art International* 8 (March 20, 1964): 50–55. Translation of introduction to *Amerikansk Pop-Kunst.* Stockholm: Moderna Museet, 1964.

————, and Mulas, Ugo. "Segal." In *New York: The New Art Scene.* New York: Holt, Rinehart, Winston, 1967, pp. 270–89.

Stevens, Mark. "Color Them Masters." *Newsweek,* February 14, 1977, pp. 80–81. Discussion of Jim Dine and George Segal.

————, and McGuigan, Cathleen. "Kent State Memorial." *Newsweek,* September 11, 1978, p. 99.

"The Super Micro-Macro World of Wonderama," *Time,* December 17, 1965, pp. 68–74.

"They Paint; You Recognize." *Time,* April 3, 1964, p. 74.

Tuchman, Phyllis. "George Segal." *Art International* 12 (September 20, 1968): 51–53.

————. "Art That Turns Life Inside Out." *Smithsonian* 28 (January 1998): 54–62.

van de Marck, Jan. "George Segal: Depersonalized Figures." In *Eight Sculptors: The Ambiguous Image.* Minneapolis: Walker Art Center, 1966, pp. 26–29.

————. "George Segal: Love's Labors Cast." *Playboy* 18 (December 1971): 195–200, 259–60.

————. "Spatial Dialectics in the Sculpture of George Segal." *Artscanada* 29 (spring 1972): 35–38.

Wohlfert, Lee. "Sculptor George Segal Is Still Art's Master of Plaster." *People,* March 14, 1977, pp. 78–80.

Zona, Louis. "A Segal Comes to Youngstown." *Dialogue: The Ohio Arts Journal,* July–August 1980, pp. 12–14.

Films

American Art in the Sixties. Barbara Rose and Michael Blackwood. New York: Blackwood Productions, 1973, 57 minutes.

American Art in the Sixties, Part I: The Pioneers (George Segal, narrator). *Part III: The New World.* Michael Blackwood. New York: Blackwood Productions, 1978, each part, 58 minutes.

Artists of New Jersey: George Segal. New York: WNET/Channel 13 telecast, July 22, 1969. On deposit, Museum of Modern Art Film Library, 28 minutes.

The Artist's Studio: Meyer Schapiro Visits George Segal. Michael Blackwood. New York: Blackwood Productions, 1982, 28 minutes.

George Segal. Michael Blackwood. New York: Blackwood Productions, 1979, 58 minutes.

Index

The photographers and the sources of photographic material other than those indicated in the captions are as follows: Courtesy of the artist: plates 12, 15, 114; Geoffrey Clements, New York (courtesy Sidney Janis Gallery): plates 14, 33, 41, 43, 79; D. James Dee, New York (courtesy Sidney Janis Gallery): plates 76, 77; Allan Finkelman, New York (courtesy Sidney Janis Gallery): frontispiece, plates 6, 9, 13, 51–53, 71, 72, 87, 89, 104–7, 115, 116; Willa Heider, Boston: plate 109; O. E. Nelson, New York: plates 17, 32, 73, 74, 98; O. E. Nelson, New York (courtesy Sidney Janis Gallery): plates 3, 27, 47, 68, 75, 78, 81, 82, 86, 91, 92, 95, 100, 102, 103; Eric Pollitzer, New York (courtesy Sidney Janis Gallery): plates 30, 45, 46, 61, 69, 70, 108; David Preston, Southampton, New York: plate 11; Nathan Rabin, New York (courtesy Sidney Janis Gallery): plates 28, 58; Juhani Riekola, Tampere, Finland: plate 62; George Roos, New York: front cover, plate 48; Courtesy Sidney Janis Gallery, New York: plates 10, 22, 24, 29, 42, 54–56, 66, 83, 90, 101; Walker Art Center, Minneapolis: plates 8, 19.

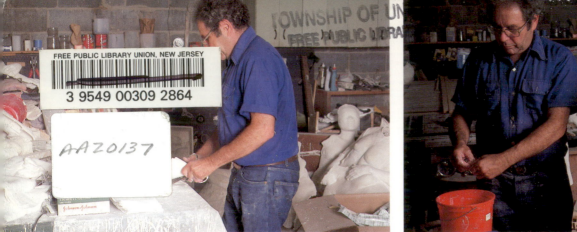

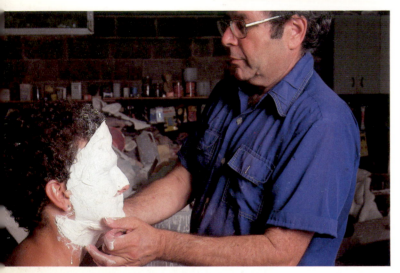

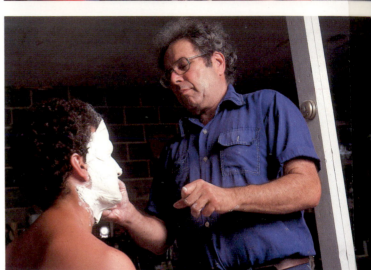

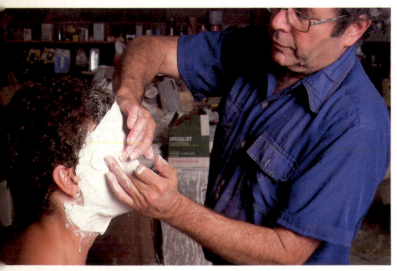

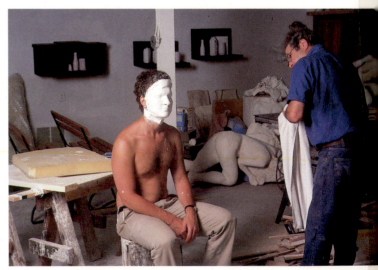

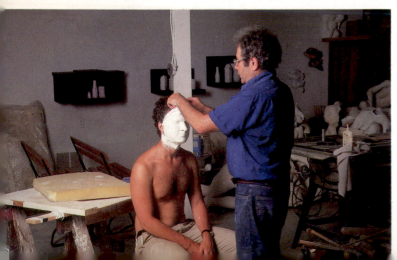

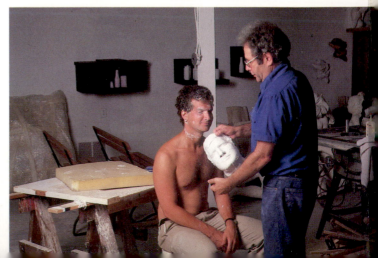